Amoris Laetitia and the Spirit of Vatican II

"In the context of one of contemporary Catholicism's most contentious debates, this work helpfully presents the differing interpretations of *Amoris Laetitia*. At the same time Biliniewicz successfully argues that these interpretations have a correlate with how the documents of Vatican II were received in differing ways. Highly recommended."

Paul Morrissey, *President of Campion College, Australia*

*Amoris Laetiti*a, Pope Francis' post-synodal exhortation on love in the family, turned out to be one of the most controversial documents of the Magisterium of the Catholic Church in recent decades. It was published in April 2016 following the two "Synods of Bishops on the Family" held in 2014 and 2015. The document brought division amongst the Catholic hierarchy, theologians and pastors, and nearly two years after its publication its exact meaning and its implications for the Church are still a matter of dispute. A number of prelates present at the two Synods indicated that these gatherings were animated by "the spirit of Vatican II." This work links the notion of "the spirit of Vatican II" with *Amoris Laetitia* and it argues that a hermeneutics of interpretation of the Second Vatican Council which focuses on following "the spirit of the Council" is the hermeneutics which can be, and in the future most likely will be, the predominant way of interpreting and implementing *Amoris Laetitia*.

This book aims to provide a contribution to this hotly debated topic in the field of Catholic theology.

Mariusz Biliniewicz is Associate Dean and Senior Lecturer in Theology at the University of Notre Dame, Australia.

Routledge Focus on Religion

Amoris Laetitia and the Spirit of Vatican II
The Source of Controversy
Mariusz Biliniewicz

For more information about this series, please visit: www.routledge.com/
Routledge-Focus-on-Religion/book-series/RFR

Amoris Laetitia and the
Spirit of Vatican II
The Source of Controversy

Mariusz Biliniewicz

Routledge
Taylor & Francis Group

LONDON AND NEW YORK

First published 2018 by Routledge
2 Park Square, Milton Park, Abingdon, Oxfordshire OX14 4RN
52 Vanderbilt Avenue, New York, NY 10017

Routledge is an imprint of the Taylor & Francis Group, an informa business

First issued in paperback 2020

British Library Cataloguing-in-Publication Data
A catalogue record for this book is available from the British Library

Library of Congress Cataloging-in-Publication Data
Names: Biliniewicz, Mariusz, 1981– author.
Title: Amoris laetitia and the spirit of Vatican II : the source of controversy / Mariusz Biliniewicz.
Description: 1 [edition]. | New York : Routledge, 2018. | Includes bibliographical references and index.
Identifiers: LCCN 2018009032 | ISBN 9780815382560 (hardback) | ISBN 9781351201919 (ebook)
Subjects: LCSH: Vatican Council (2nd : 1962–1965 : Basilica di San Pietro in Vaticano) | Catholic Church. Pope (2013– : Francis). Amoris laetitia. | Families—Religious aspects—Catholic Church. | Catholic Church—Doctrines.
Classification: LCC BX830 1962 .B495 2018 | DDC 261.8/ 358088282—dc23
LC record available at https://lccn.loc.gov/2018009032

ISBN: 978-0-8153-8256-0 (hbk)
ISBN: 978-0-367-60698-5 (pbk)

Typeset in Times New Roman
by Apex CoVantage, LLC

Contents

Introduction

The post-synodal apostolic exhortation *Amoris Laetitia* (*AL*)[1] signed by Pope Francis on 19 March 2016 and published on 8 April 2016 is a result of his reflections on the proceedings of the Third Extraordinary General Assembly of the Synod of Bishops and the Fourteenth Ordinary General Assembly of the Synod of Bishops. These gatherings took place between 5 and 19 October 2014 and 4 and 25 October 2015, respectively, and are sometimes referred to as one event: "the Synod(s) of Bishops on the Family." The two sessions in a natural way sparked some significant interest not only among Catholic observers and theologians, but also among non-Catholics, including the wider public. This general interest in issues which are internal to the Catholic community is, at least partially, a result of the way Pope Francis is often being presented in the popular mass media: a courageous and radical reformer trying to renew the Catholic Church according to the guidelines provided by the Second Vatican Council (1962–65). According to a well-known narrative, the work of renewal initiated by Pope John XXIII (1958–63), the Pope who convoked the Council but died after its first session, was only partially taken up and carried forward by his immediate successor, Paul VI (1963–78), and after a very short pontificate of John Paul I (1978) it was, at least in some respects, halted by the pontificates of John Paul II (1978–2005) and Benedict XVI (2005–2013). It is frequently said that the last two popes not only failed to continue the initiated reforms, but in fact supported certain "restoration tendencies" in the Church and also that their "restorative reading" of the Council in practice resulted in a certain return to the pre-conciliar ways of the Church. Pope Francis is often presented as "the new John XXIII" who wishes to return to the ideas which were put forward by "the good pope" and then taken up by the Council.[2] The Catholic Church is thus presented as an institution which is undergoing, or is just about to undergo, a significant change in the way she functions, teaches and perhaps even in what she believes. One of the markers of this change was expected to be a review of the magisterial position on certain issues related to marriage and sexual ethics, such as the issues of participation of the divorced and civilly remarried Catholics in the life of the Church, the place of homosexual Catholics in pastoral practices of the Church and matters related to the spacing of children and methods of birth control. Expectations of many were high, the atmosphere surrounding the synods was intense and this often resulted in the existence of various premature and inadequate press releases about what was happening during the synods and where the Pope stood in all of this. The fact of the matter was that, apart from the opening and closing of the synod, the Pope did not say anything, and his reflections and decisions were going to be published in a post-synodal apostolic exhortation.[3]

Amoris Laetitia was signed by Francis on the third anniversary of his Inauguration Mass as Pope, and it was published nearly three weeks later. It is a long document consisting of nine chapters, 325 paragraphs and 391 footnotes, running to a total of 256 pages. It is addressed to "bishops, priests and deacons, consecrated persons, Christian married couples and all the lay faithful" and it is written in a language which is rather common for Francis, but not that common for pre-Francis magisterial documents. It is pragmatic, uncomplicated and for most part rather easily understandable even for those with little theological background. Many readers comment that the document often reads like a good retreat; a thoughtful conference; or a fine, lengthy but very profound and practical homily addressed directly to married couples.[4]

This "pastoral style," however, does not mean that the document lacks theological depth or complexity or that the interpretation of all passages contained within it is straightforward and plain. On the contrary, despite its seeming simplicity, certain parts of the exhortation prove to be very difficult to interpret, especially on those points where the expectations were greatest.[5] Chapter VIII, with which the Pope hoped to challenge everyone,[6] might be one of the most disputed portions of a magisterial document in recent decades.[7] Francis himself suggests that "rushed reading of the text" should be avoided and that "the greatest benefit . . . will come if each part [of the whole text] is read patiently and carefully."[8]

AL sums up the proceedings of two synods and relies heavily on the official *Relatio Synodi* from 2014 and *Relatio Finalis* from 2015.[9] It is neither possible nor necessary to give here even a brief account of the proceedings of the synods, especially given that this account is yet to be written by Church historians.[10] The main idea of this particular contribution to the ongoing debate was inspired by statements made by some high-ranked officials of the synods who described its proceedings as being carried out "in the spirit of Vatican II." One of the synod presidents, Cardinal Louis Tagle, said at a press conference that "some of the synod fathers and participants said openly that they felt the spirit of Vatican II very much" and that for those who did not participate in Vatican II, the synod was "a slice of it – some sort of a taste of it."[11] Archbishop Bruno Forte, the secretary of the synod, at the same conference also stated that the synod "was done in the spirit of the Second Vatican Council."[12] The two churchmen explained what they meant: Tagle (a Vatican II scholar) talked about "the spirit of listening,"[13] and Forte, referring to the opening paragraphs of Vatican II's *Gaudium et Spes* (*GS*),[14] stated that "the synod wished to hear the joys and the hopes, the griefs and the anxieties of the women and men of this age."[15] However, upon reflection it seems to the present author that the expression "in the spirit of Vatican II" can in fact betray an even deeper intuition. This work will argue that an analysis of the meaning of the phrase "the spirit of Vatican II" might reveal answers to some questions about how one might, and perhaps very often will, interpret certain passages of *AL*, especially those which are rather ambiguous and unclear and which are being understood by pastors and scholars in various, often contradictory, ways. The work will thus attempt to examine how "the spirit of Vatican II," as a hermeneutical principle for interpreting the Council, can provide insight into the search for a possible "true meaning" of *AL*.

This task be undertaken in three steps. In the first chapter, a presentation of certain widely recognised difficulties in interpreting Vatican II will be carried out. It is an interesting phenomenon that the texts of Vatican II are understood by commentators in very diverse ways and that they are used for both supporting and rejecting various changes which occurred in the Roman Catholic Church in the decades that followed the Council. This diversity of interpretations is often attributed to the presence of obscurities, ambiguities and compromise formulas in the conciliar texts which allegedly were placed there in order to win the Council's fathers' consensus needed for passing the documents.

In the second chapter, a hermeneutics of Vatican II based on the notion of following "the spirit of Vatican II" will be explained and two important elements of the hermeneutics will be presented. The first element is "creative fidelity" and it amounts to considering the innovative elements contained in the text as *the* key to interpretation of the Council. The second element is the emphasis on the *style* in which the documents of Vatican II are written, since not only *what* the Council says, but *how* it says it is vital for its interpretation (the Council was "a linguistic event").

In the third chapter, an application of the two hermeneutical keys identified in the second chapter will be attempted with regard to *AL* in the search for a possible "proper way" of understanding this document and its meaning for the Church. An argument will be made that reading *AL* with "creative fidelity" and emphasising it as a "linguistic event" can be, and presumably will be, used as the most common hermeneutical keys in interpretation of this document, especially by those who understand it as a ground-breaking paradigm shift for Catholic theology. It needs to be acknowledged that the topic of interpretation and implementation of *AL* is very lively and that writing about such a "moving target" is always burdened with risk of the final product being not as up to date as it would be desired. While every effort was made to utilise sources available at the time of writing, no guarantee can be given that at the time of publication of this work some new developments will not arise and reshape or redirect the current discussion. However, it is believed that regardless of these possible new developments, the main argument of this work, that is, that "the spirit of Vatican II" can be found in *AL* and will be employed in the process of interpreting and implementing it, will still stand.

Notes

1 Pope Francis, *Amoris Laetitia* (19 March 2016), 7, w2.vatican.va/content/dam/ francesco/pdf/apost_exhortations/documents/papa-francesco_esortazione-ap_20160319_amoris-laetitia_en.pdf.

2 See for example Andrea Tornielli, "Pope Francis: The New John XXIII?," *La Stampa* (3 June 2013), www.lastampa.it/2013/06/03/esteri/vatican-insider/en/ pope-francis-the-new-john-xxiii-O5YQamutYpzvELP3YcEBAJ/pagina.html. Christopher Lamb, referring to Cardinal Cormac Murphy-O'Connor, speaks about Francis as "the man to breathe life back into the stalled reforms of Vatican II" and argues that "[t]he legacy of Francis, it is becoming increasingly clear, will be a papacy that reinvigorated the spirit of the Council in the life of the Church," see his "Francis on the Front Foot," *The Tablet* (30 September 2017): 4–5, at 4. Naturally, not all commentators embrace this view and many choose to read the recent history of the Catholic Church, including Vatican II and the papacies of Paul VI, John Paul II, Benedict XVI and Francis through the lenses of greater, underlying continuity. More will be said about this in the following chapters.

3 Thomas Knieps-Port le Roi and Roger Burggraeve, "New Wine in New Wineskins: *Amoris Laetitia* and the Church's Teaching on Marriage and Family," *Louvain Studies* 39 (2015–16): 284–302, at 284 state about *AL* that "[p]robably no other official church document has been awaited so impatiently and with such great expectations by so many Catholics."

4 See for example Frances Correia, "My Personal Experience of Marriage and Amoris Laetitia," *Jesuit Institute South Africa* (15 April 2016), www.jesuitinstitute.org.za/ index.php/2016/04/15/my-personal-experience-of-marriage-and-amoris-laetitia/. On the other hand, Paige E. Hochschild, "A Balancing Act: Reading 'Amoris Laetitia'," *Commonweal* (20 May 2016): 15–16, at 15 complains that "*Amoris Laetitia* is a long and sometimes frustrating document," and that "[s]ome of the pope's language, while familiar, is not particularly helpful."

5 Marc Ouellet, "Accompanying, Discerning, Integrating Weakness," *L'Osservatore Romano* (21 November 2017), www.osservatoreromano.va/en/news/accompanying-discerning-integrating-weakness. See also his "A Missionary Gaze: Understanding 'Amoris Laetitia'," *L'Osservatore Romano* (8 November 2017),

www.osservatoreromano.va/en/news/missionary-gaze; Arnaud Join-Lambert, "Accompanying, Discerning and Integrating the Fragility of Couples: Pastors and Theologians at a Crossroads," in *A Point of No Return? Amoris Laetitia on Marriage, Divorce and Remarriage*, ed. Thomas Knieps-Port le Roi (Berlin: Lit Verlag, 2017), 146.

6 *AL* 7.
7 Nicholas Austin, "Not All Is Black and White," *The Tablet* (8 April 2017): 8–9, at 8.
8 *AL* 7.
9 In fact, the majority of references in *AL* are taken from these two documents. Both of them are available on the Vatican web page, www.vatican.va/roman_curia/synod/documents/rc_synod_doc_20141018_relatio-synodi-familia_en.html and www.vatican.va/roman_curia/synod/documents/rc_synod_doc_2015 1026_relazione-finale-xiv-assemblea_en.html.
10 To the date, the only work in English on the history of the two synods is Edward Pentin, *The Rigging of a Vatican Synod? An Investigation into Alleged Manipulation at the Extraordinary Synod on the Family* (San Francisco: Ignatius Press, 2015).
11 Joshua J. McElwee, "Prelates: Synod Document Is the Fruit of Vatican II Spirit," *National Catholic Reporter* (13 October 2014), www.ncronline.org/news/vatican/prelates-synod-document-fruit-vatican-ii-spirit.
12 Ibid.
13 "Listening to the Word of God; listening to the voices of the pastors and the churches that they represent; listening to not only the success stories but also to the wounds and the failures," see Louis Tagle, "The Spirit of the Synod is a Spirit of Listening," *Salt and Light Media* (15 October 2014), http://saltand lighttv.org/blogfeed/getpost.php?id=59095&language.
14 Second Vatican Council, "Pastoral Constitution on the Church in the Modern World," *Gaudium et spes* (7 December 1965), www.vatican.va/archive/hist_councils/ii_vatican_council/documents/vat-ii_const_19651207_gaudium-et-spes_en.html.
15 McElwee, "Prelates: Synod Document Is the Fruit of Vatican II Spirit."

1 Difficulties in interpreting Vatican II

While there is no shortage of various, often contrasting, evaluations of the Second Vatican Council,[1] one thing that all sides of the debate hold in common is that Vatican II was an unprecedented event of remarkable importance in modern Church history and that its influence on the Roman Catholic Church cannot be understated. James Hitchcock called it "the most important event within the Church in the past four hundred years,"[2] Emile Poulat stated that the Church had changed more in that decade that it had in the previous century[3] and Joseph A. Komonchak commented that "there are very few features of everyday Catholic life, from the central elements of its preaching and worship to the most peripheral of its etiquettes, that were not affected by the Council or at least by the changes said to have been introduced as a consequence or implementation of it."[4] Whichever hermeneutics of the Council is applied and whatever the opinion about the reforms prescribed and those actually carried out, there is no doubt that something really important happened in the Church, and that something was a result of Vatican II.[5]

Apart from different opinions about *what* actually happened at the Council and in its aftermath (what kind of changes did Vatican II advocate? which changes were introduced?), whether those changes adequately reflected the Council's wishes (did they go too far or did they fail to go far enough?) or whether their results were positive or negative, there is also some pluralism regarding *how* these changes actually took place.

This issue touches on the question of the hermeneutics of the Council and the manner of implementing reforms after the Council. An increasing number of scholars[6] argue that many of the post–Vatican II reforms in the Church resulted from illegitimate and exaggerated over-interpretations of the conciliar texts in which those reforms find little or no grounding. The responsibility for those misinterpretations, they argue, is not to be attributed to the Council itself, but to certain interpretations of the Council – interpretations which, according to representatives of this view, go against the intentions of the popes who convoked and closed the Council and against the intentions of the fathers of the Council, who did not mandate revolutions, but rather careful, moderate reforms.[7] This way of understanding the relationship between Vatican II and post-conciliar reforms is often based on the important, in the view of its proponents, distinction between "the letter of the Council" (what the Council actually said) and "the spirit of the Council" (a "message" which the Council as a whole conveys and which extends beyond the mere texts). Insistence on the latter is often blamed for de-emphasising and consequently distorting the former. Representatives of this view do not dismiss completely the notion of "the spirit of Vatican II," but strongly argue that if one wishes to discover this spirit, one cannot find it anywhere except in the texts of Vatican II. It is only in the officially promulgated, final documents of the Council that one can find answer to the question of the intentions, the meaning and the orientation of the Council.[8] Once what Vatican II really said is replaced with what we would like it to have said, or with what we think it should have said, or with what we think the presumptive Third Vatican Council should say, the true meaning of "the spirit of Vatican II" is distorted and turned into a "spectre"[9] or even "anti-spirit."[10]

There are, however, scholars who see things differently. While they do not deny that some of the post–Vatican II reforms were not immediately successful and acknowledge that perhaps some of them were too hastily implemented and poorly conducted, they argue that the overall picture of the Church after the Council is still far more positive than before it. They see the most important post-conciliar reforms and developments not as distortions and over-interpretations of the Council, but as actual realisations of its mandates. While they would tend to agree that not all of the post–Vatican II developments were desired by the Council *explicitly*, since providing explicit instructions was not the Council's purpose, these developments were contained in its texts at least *implicitly*. Even if they are not mandated directly by the conciliar texts in the set form in which they stand, they can be derived indirectly through reading the mind and the general orientation of the Council. They argue that this "general orientation" is not something invented in order to repress the actual texts, but it is to be found precisely *in* the texts. These scholars would concur, therefore, with the principle of not separating "the spirit of the Council" from "the letter of the Council" (a principle endorsed by the 1985 Synod of Bishops devoted to Vatican II), but would assert that a careful and honest reading of the texts, especially in the context of preceding magisterial writings, cannot overlook the overall shift which these documents represent.[11] Both groups would, therefore, recognise not only the validity of the principle of not separating the spirit from the letter, but also the need to derive the spirit from the letter. At the same time, however, they draw different conclusions from the same letter and understand the meaning of the Council differently, both in its general character and in its particular enactments.

The fact that both those who generally cherish the post-conciliar reforms and those who criticise them find justification for their positions in the same texts of the Council is no small difficulty for the interpreter of Vatican II. Why do scholars and pastors looking at the same documents derive such contrasting conclusions from them? The problem of interpretation cannot be resolved simply by referring to the hierarchy of the documents of the Council and stating that certain documents (usually constitutions) have precedence over others (declarations and decrees), since the problem concerns also the inner dynamics and hermeneutics of particular documents: Is there a hierarchy *among* the four constitutions? Among the nine declarations? Among the three decrees? Is there a hierarchy of chapters and statements within the documents themselves? If there is a tension between various parts of the particular document, could one part be considered more important than another? And if so, on what grounds?[12]

A good example of these kinds of hermeneutical problems is the liturgy. Those who are generally satisfied with the post-conciliar liturgical reforms of Pope Paul VI point to the conciliar Constitution on the Sacred Liturgy *Sacrosanctum Concilium*[13] (*SC*) and to those passages which, in their judgment, mandate the reforms which were carried out. They mention such principles as the adaptation to the needs of the time (*SC* 1), ecumenism (*SC* 1), the elimination from the liturgy of those elements which are outdated and unsuitable (*SC* 21), the simplification and curtailing of rites for the sake of noble simplicity (*SC* 34), the fostering of active participation (*SC* 30, 50),[14] making the liturgy more immediately understandable (*SC* 34), the elimination of "useless repetitions" (*SC* 34), inculturation (*SC* 38), looking at the early Christian liturgy as the ideal to be strived for (*SC* 50) and the carrying out of the reform in a relatively short period of time (*SC* 25 states that "the liturgical books are to be revised as soon as possible"). There is no doubt that the post–Vatican II reform was carried out with many of these principles in mind. These principles, it is argued, are not just inspired by some vague and unidentified "spirit of the Council," but are derived from the very texts of the Constitution. To question them means to question not only the particular implementation of the reform, not only the "spirit," but also the "letter" of the Council.[15]

Those who take a more critical view of the liturgical reform do not see things in the same way and are not ready to acknowledge with the same ease that the reform was simply a realisation of the Council's wishes. They look at the same Constitution on the Sacred Liturgy, but see and emphasise passages which, in their judgment, not only do not mandate many practices adopted in the Roman Catholic liturgy after the Council, but which are in evident opposition to them. They argue that nowhere in the Constitution can one find provisions for such changes as complete elimination of Latin and the entire vernacularisation of the liturgy (in fact *SC* 36 states that "the use of the Latin language . . . is to be preserved in the Latin rites"), the changing of the orientation of the celebrant from *ad orientem* to *versus populum*, the introduction of the practice of receiving Communion in the hand, the replacing of Gregorian chant with popular hymns (*SC* 116 states that the chant "should be given pride of place in liturgical services") or the creation of new Eucharistic Prayers. On the other hand, the document states that "there must be no innovations unless the good of the Church genuinely and certainly requires them; and care must be taken that any new forms adopted should in some way grow organically from forms already existing" (*SC* 23). This suggests, according to them, that the Council fathers did not envisage any radical reform, but rather a careful, slow, organic renovation. To these authors, criticisms of the liturgical reform are not just some form of some alleged nostalgic, conservative and anti-conciliar bias, but rather an attempt to remain faithful to the wishes of the Council expressed in the text of *SC*.

Tensions such as these can be found not only in *SC*, but in many other, perhaps even all, documents of Vatican II. Examples include the tensions between the teaching on papacy and collegiality of bishops (*Lumen Gentium*), between the state's obligations toward the truth and the true religion and the principle of religious liberty (*Dignitatis Humanae*), between the uniqueness of the role and mission of the Catholic Church and the role of other Christian denominations and even non-Christian religions in God's plan (*Unitatis Redintegratio* and *Nostra Aetate*). The existence of these tensions caused Walter Kasper to state that "both conservatives and progressives can find support in individual conciliar statements"[16] and John O'Malley, S.J. to conclude that "somewhere in the documents of the council can be found a line to support almost every conceivable theological position."[17]

How can this difficulty be resolved? By merely looking at the texts, is it possible to say that one side got the text right and the other one wrong? Many reject such a manner of reading the Council's documents and consider it "proof-reading," that is, looking for justification for certain views and positions in the given text, quite independently of the text's context and the history of its development. Those who reject this kind of "proof-reading" believe that any side of the debate will get the Council wrong if it is going to look only at the text. This is because the Council's documents were not intended to resolve all theological disputes and practical matters, but only to indicate the current state of the question, open paths for further developments and indicate routes which may be pursued in the future. Rather than being the last word on the matter, the texts are really only a beginning. The "spirit of the Council," thus, *is* contained in the letter, but it also transcends it; while it cannot be divorced from the letter, it cannot also be limited to the letter alone. This hermeneutics of the Council needs to be explained in greater detail in the following chapter because it can shed some light on the problems related to the diversity of interpretations of *AL*.

Notes

1 A short overview of these can be found in Massimo Faggioli, *Vatican II: The Battle for Meaning* (New York: Paulist Press, 2012), *passim*, but especially chapters 1 and 2.
2 James Hitchcock, *Catholicism and Modernity: Confrontation or Capitulation* (New York: Seabury Press, 1979), 75.
3 Emile Poulat, *Une Eglise ébranlée: Chamgement, conflit et continuité de Pie XII à Jean Paul II* (Paris: Casterman, 1980), 41.
4 Joseph A. Komonchak, "Interpreting the Council: Catholic Attitudes toward Vatican II," in *Being Right: Conservative Catholics in America*, eds. Mary Jo Weaver and R. Scott Appleby (Bloomington: Indiana University Press, 1995), 17–36, at 17; the previous two references are taken from Komonchak's work.
5 Faggioli, *Vatican II: The Battle for Meaning*, notes that "no one disputes the epoch – making impact of Vatican II" (p. 1) and calls Vatican II a "major turning point" (p. 9).
6 Increasing especially since 2005, that is, since the election of Cardinal Joseph Ratzinger to the Chair of Peter, a churchman and theologian who has argued for a long time that implementation of Vatican II needs revisiting and that it deserves a critical evaluation in the light of the actual wishes and intentions of the Council.
7 Peter Steinfels, *A People Adrift: The Crisis of the Roman Catholic Church in America* (New York: Simon & Schuster, 2003), 32–39 describes this hermeneutical stream as "conservative" and juxtaposes it with the "ultraconservative" one (which says that Vatican II itself is responsible for the post-conciliar crisis due to errors it contains), the "liberal" (which says that Vatican II initiated reforms of which many have been successfully implemented, but even more work is needed) and the "ultraliberal" (which says that Vatican II was betrayed in the post-conciliar era through giving in to conservative forces). Faggioli adopts this schema and elaborates on it in his "Vatican II: History and Narratives," *Theological Studies* 73 (2012): 749–767, especially at 753–759.
8 Most prominent representatives of this view include the founders of the *Communio* group (Henri de Lubac, Joseph Ratzinger, Hans Urs von Balthasar) and some more contemporary writers such as Agostino Marchetto, *The Second Vatican Ecumenical Council: A Counterpoint for the History of the Council*, trans. Kenneth D. Whitehead (Chicago, IL: University of Scranton Press, 2010) or Matthew L. Lamb and Matthew Levering and the many scholars who contributed to their *Vatican II: Renewal within Tradition* (Oxford/New York: Oxford University Press, 2008).
9 Joseph Cardinal Ratzinger, *Principles of Catholic Theology: Building Stones for a Fundamental Theology*, trans. Sister Mary Frances McCarthy, S.N.D. (San Francisco: Ignatius Press, 1987), 390.
10 *Konzils-Ungeist* in German, see Joseph Cardinal Ratzinger with Vittorio Messori, *The Ratzinger Report: An Exclusive Interview on the State of the Church*, trans. Salvator Attanasio and Graham Harrison (San Francisco: Ignatius Press, 1985), 34.

11 More detailed description of this position and examples of scholars who adopt it will be given in the following chapter.

12 For a good overview of the positions in this discussions see Faggioli, *Vatican II: The Battle for Meaning*, 125–133.

13 Second Vatican Council, "Constitution on the Sacred Liturgy," *Sacrosanctum Concilium* (4 December 1963), www.vatican.va/archive/hist_councils/ ii_vatican_council/documents/vat-ii_const_19631204_sacrosanctum-concilium_ en.html

14 "Active participation" understood here not only in the spiritual way (internal connection with what is being celebrated), which is the aspect authors such as Klaus Gamber or Joseph Ratzinger strongly emphasise, but also in terms of external activities carried out by the faithful during the celebration. *SC* gives examples of such external participation: "acclamations, responses, psalmody, antiphons, and songs, as well as by actions, gestures, and bodily attitudes" (*SC* 30).

15 For more about this discussion see Mariusz Biliniewicz, "Sacrosanctum Concilium: A Review of the Theological Critique," in *Sacrosanctum Concilium: Sacred Liturgy and the Second Vatican Council: Proceedings of the Sixth Fota International Liturgical Conference, 2013: Essays in Commemoration of the Fiftieth Anniversary of the Promulgation of the Conciliar Constitution: 1963–2013*, ed. John M. Cunningham, O.P. (Wells, Somerset: Smenos, 2015), 71–90.

16 Walter Kasper, *Theology and Church* (New York: Crossroad, 1989), 170.

17 John O'Malley, "Erasmus and Vatican II: Interpreting the Council," in *Cristianesimo nella storia. Saggi in onore di Giuseppe Alberigo*, eds. Alberto Melloni, Daniele Menozzi and Maria Paola Toschi (Bologna: Il Mulino, 1996), 195–211, at 197.

2   The spirit and style of Vatican II

In this chapter, the hermeneutical key of following "the spirit of Vatican II" will be explained in greater detail. It will be argued that two pivotal elements of this hermeneutics can be identified and applied in the task of trying to interpret *AL*.

The first element consists of downplaying the traditional teaching and emphasising novelties in those conciliar formulas which contain both the classical formulations and impulses to the new. It also consists of adopting "creative fidelity" in reading of the text, that is, in going beyond the texts themselves and following their general orientation.

The second element consists of emphasising the importance of abandoning the traditional language used by the magisterial documents before the Council and the adoption of a new language in which the Council decided to teach. As said before, it appears that these two hermeneutical principles identified in the process of interpretation of Vatican II can be easily linked also to the interpretation of *AL*.

2.1. Ambiguities in the texts – towards "creative fidelity"

The Second Vatican Council differed in many ways from the previous councils of the Church. One of the main differences is the language the Council adopted – language which is less precise, more open-ended and which results in the creation of certain tensions and ambiguities in the documents. According to a common narrative, these tensions and ambiguities are the results of compromises which the drafters of the documents needed to make in order to gain unanimity among the conciliar fathers who would vote on them. It is said that since Vatican II was the largest gathering of the leaders of the Church in history and also the first meeting of the "world Church" – that is, of bishops from all continents, languages and cultures – diversity of views could be expected and needed to be managed. This diversity became more and more evident as the Council progressed and the authors of the documents were becoming increasingly aware of how difficult it was going to be to produce texts which would be approved by the whole gathering.[1] O'Malley talks about a "lack of clarity" and "vagueness and indeterminacy" which often softens the documents' language and, thus, their whole message.[2] He also calls the Council documents "committee documents, full of compromise and deliberate ambiguity."[3] Herman J. Pottmeyer detects an "internal incoherence of the conciliar texts,"[4] and Ormond Rush talks about "clear compromises, ambiguities, and juxtaposition of conflicting viewpoints."[5] The presence of these brings Rush to the conclusion that "the conflicting camps or forces at work among the bishops remain coded in the documents."[6] Rush argues that "ecclesial unanimity was achieved . . . *through the retention of conflicting attitudes*" (emphasis original) and, following Otto Hermann Pesch, asserts that while "with texts of the ecclesial magisterium one is always dealing with compromise formulae," in the case of Vatican II we are dealing with a *deliberate* compromise and ambiguity which Pesch calls "contradictory pluralism."[7] This "contradictory pluralism . . . sets in tension two positions, *leaving the issue open for future synthesis*" (emphasis original).[8] This "juxtaposition of elements of the old with the new . . . itself, was a development" since it introduced into the official Church documents something which was not there before, and it left the "future interpreters the creative task of reception, that is, finishing off the job of arriving at a new synthesis that could not be achieved at the time."[9] This understanding of the inner dynamics between the old and the new present in the conciliar documents sees Vatican II as "unfinished business"[10] demanding "new synthesis"[11] which will go beyond the debates that shaped these middle-ground formulas and which will be carried forward in the same spirit of creativity. In sum, "what was written with imagination must be read with imagination."[12]

Pottmeyer, Pesch and Rush are not the only scholars who detect the existence of ambiguities and lack of coherence in at least some of the conciliar documents. Joseph Ratzinger also detected some "inner tensions" – tensions which, however inevitable, allowed "for the balance of the conciliar document to be disrupted one-sidedly in a specific direction."[13] Richard R. Gaillardetz agrees and believes that the ultimate disadvantage of the "method of juxtaposition" was that after the Council it enabled "various ideological camps to appeal to certain passages that appeared to support their particular ecclesiastical agenda."[14] Walter Kasper mentions scholars who see in the texts "a juxtaposition, a double viewpoint, a dialectic, if not actually a contradiction."[15] O'Malley asserts that "the unclarities, the hesitations, the qualifications, the ambivalences that mark the documents reflect the huge committee in which they were hammered out."[16] He states that since "they were the price paid to obtain consensus," their interpretation "is even more susceptible of manipulation than most other reform documents in the history of the Christian Church, especially as we move away from the event itself."[17] Roger Aubert asserts that "numerous ambiguities remain in the text, where traditional statements are melded with innovative ones," and he complains that these statements "are simply juxtaposed with each other rather than being truly integrated."[18] He concludes that "such a lack of coherence often produces divergent interpretations, with the result that some passages came to be unilaterally insisted upon more than other passages."[19] A similar position is held by Cardinal Louis Tagle, president of the 2014–15 synods. In his historical analysis dealing with the week of 16–21 November 1964, he writes that "minority questioning and strategies during the 'Black Week' brought out to light the ambiguities of the documents of the Council, but accommodating the minority positions also increased the theological compromises in the texts."[20] He explains that "the compromises in *LG* [*Lumen Gentium*] have left the doctrine of collegiality vague enough for it to be acceptable to people of different persuasions. Often conflicting ideas could find their respective justification in the same document."[21] Alessandro Rovati recognises the existence of "creative tension that can be found throughout the council documents" but also complains that in the post–Vatican II era this creative tension "has not always been properly understood and faithfully followed."[22]

Similar conclusions can be found in the work of the non-Catholic observer George Lindbeck, in his book from 1970, which carries a foreword by Catholic bishop B. C. Butler.[23] Butler states in his introduction that in the conciliar documents one can find "an element of compromise in their contents, and they represent the aspect of an unfinished dialogue between two contrasted theological 'schools', one 'conservative' and the other 'progressive.'"[24] Lindbeck takes the matter further and argues that "Vatican II represents a transitional phase in a movement which began long before it was convoked and will continue to develop far into the future."[25] He continues by saying that

> like all transitional events it is an amalgam of the new and the old. Its documents are often compromises between stale and tired ways of thinking and fresh and vital ones. Sometimes they are even deliberately ambiguous; the only way to rally a consensus from bishops of all parties was to clothe the new in old language (or the old in new language) so that what was said would at least be tolerable, even if not satisfying, to both conservatives and progressives.[26]

Avery Dulles, S.J. came to similar conclusions when he stated:

> The council fathers, under the direction of Pope Paul VI, made every effort to achieve unanimity and express the consensus of the whole episcopate, not the ideas of one particular school. For this reason, they

sought to harmonize differing views, without excluding any significant minority. In some cases they adopted deliberate ambiguities.[27]

These tensions and ambiguities cause difficulties with the interpretation of the texts. For Lindbeck, however, and also for a significant number of Catholic theologians, the solution to the dilemma of finding the correct interpretation of the texts is obvious: the interpreter should avoid "simply taking them [the texts of the Council] as they stand" or "repeating or summarizing them." Rather, he or she should focus on "the *new* [emphasis original] theological emphases which are likely to prove most significant as a basis and guide for further developments."[28] Antonio Ascerbi states that the interpreter who wants to be faithful to the Council must go beyond it because the Council recognised its own limits and historicity and could only initiate a process of reform.[29] Being faithful to the Council requires going "beyond the actual conciliar texts themselves"[30] and engaging in interpretation "with the same Spirit-inspired creativity that it itself exhibited."[31] It is not possible to talk about *one* meaning of the Council since it is possible that

> there is more to the "meaning" of a text than what its authors explicitly intended to say. Future generations may find things in Vatican II that go beyond what the authors intended, but which are thoroughly in accord with the spirit and the letter of the Council.[32]

Since "a text is dead until it is read,"[33] there is a great weight of responsibility on the receiver of the conciliar texts. Rush explains that since "it is the receiver who brings the documents into realisation" it means that he or she can and should not only "*make* sense of them" (emphasis original), that is, not only find their meaning, but also "give meaning to them." This means that "the receiver is a co-creator of the meaning of what is communicated. Hence the appropriated meaning could legitimately go beyond the original authorial intention." Rush concludes that "the original authors 'need' future readers to make sense of a text whose authors may not have had those future contexts in mind."[34]

Thus, according to the proponents of this view, a sound reading of the Council includes not only the adoption of a correct "hermeneutics of the texts" (which is what Benedict XVI et al. insist on), but also a consideration of the "hermeneutics of the authors" and the "hermeneutics of the receivers."[35] With regard to the "hermeneutics of the authors," Faggioli states that focusing on the texts of the Council without taking into account the whole process by which they emerged, the intention of the authors and the general orientation of the Council represents "a scant understanding of the profound nature of that moment" and concludes that the "interpretation of Vatican II as an exercise of textual exegesis made in a historical vacuum is . . . the subtlest form of rejection of the council."[36] O'Malley holds a similar opinion and argues that "only by tracing the documents' genesis and, ever more important, locating them in their contexts can their deeper significance be made clear."[37] He states that the "myopic, sometimes almost proof-texting, approach to the council that focuses on the wording of the documents without regard for contexts, without regard for before and after, and without regard for vocabulary and literary form" often results in "a minimal interpretation of the council, an interpretation that fails to see the council as the new moment it wanted to be in the history of the Catholic Church."[38]

There are writers who are troubled by the presence of incoherencies and ambiguities in the conciliar documents. Giuseppe Dossetti, for example, acknowledges the existence of "mistakes, compromises, and ambiguities" in the texts of Vatican II, but at the same time he asserts that "the Spirit works despite any mistake or any lack of human clarity."[39] He argues, nevertheless, that it is necessary "to do everything we can to eliminate these obstacles" for "any lack of clarity of thought certainly does not serve the things of the Spirit."[40] Romano Amerio complains that the ambiguities in the conciliar texts meant that in practice "the spirit of the council outstripped the council itself" and that in the post–Vatican II era various ideas and intentions were ascribed to the Council without sufficient grounding in its actual texts.[41] Michael Davies goes even further and calls the ambiguities contained in the texts "time bombs" which were built into the conciliar documents only to be detonated later by those of progressive orientation.[42]

However, there are also authors who consider the juxtapositions and internal tensions in the conciliar documents to be an advantage. While Dossetti argued that the Holy Spirit can work *despite* the lack of clarity, others seems to suggest that he can work *through* that lack of clarity.[43] If this is the case, then the tension in the conciliar documents between the old and the new can be understood to be precisely *the* locus of the development which the Council brought about. It is the impulses toward the new that express best the mind of the Council, and it is in them that the Council's spirit can be found.

Authors who favour this way of interpreting Vatican II are usually of the opinion that in order to understand the Council properly, conciliar texts need to be analysed in a broader context. This broader context consists first of looking at all texts of the Council as a unity. Rush, recalling the principles of intertextuality, compares the corpus of texts of Vatican II to that of the Bible and the internal unity which needs to be kept in mind when interpreting it. Recalling the hermeneutical principles offered by the 1985 Synod of

Bishops[44] he states that the conciliar documents, "once produced . . . are to be seen not in isolation, but in terms of one another."[45] Faggioli also argues that "Vatican II has a theological integrity; minimizing one document minimizes all the documents."[46] O'Malley states similarly that the conciliar documents "form a coherent corpus, and they must be interpreted accordingly"[47] and that they "are not a grab bag of discrete units. To toy with one of the documents, therefore, is to toy with all of them."[48] Gilles Routhier calls for a reading of the Council which would be "a grasp of the whole, a synthetic approach that highlights the central axes, the load-bearing structures, and the internal dynamic of each of the documents and of the global architecture governing the document's exposition."[49] Such a broad outlook "would indicate the coherence and thrust, the movement of ideas, the cross-references of texts, the connections, the ideas that appear in several documents, the nodal questions, the categories that create structures, etc."[50]

This broader context consists also of taking into account the history of the texts and the general progression of the conciliar events. It is argued that when one looks at the journey which various schemata undertook to arrive in their ultimate shape – at the discussions and modifications of the texts at different stages – it is possible to trace a certain trend, a direction, a general thrust and a guiding vision. This guiding vision or orientation which is present in the documents of Vatican II taken as a corpus and discovered through "intertextual analysis" is what is usually called "the spirit of the Council."[51]

While there is no one definition of "the spirit of the Council,"[52] for the purpose of this work John O'Malley's explanations will be used. He defines "the spirit of Vatican II" as "an orientation that goes beyond specific enactments,"[53] an overriding vision which transcends the particulars of the documents and has to be taken into account in interpreting the Council.[54]

O'Malley acknowledges that due to the presence of many deliberate ambiguities present in the conciliar texts, it is not always easy to find that *one* orientation, that *one* overriding vision. When analysing what he identifies as "the issues-under-the issues" of Vatican II,[55] O'Malley acknowledges that

> by their very nature these issues do not admit of definitive resolution one way or the other. Their essence is to be in tension. Each of them pulls in opposite direction. Both directions have validity; neither is absolute. The church, like any organization, must deal with the tension, not deny it.[56]

Yet he argues that even with this inevitable tension remaining, the Council *did* want something to happen and that through an analysis of the conciliar texts, it is possible to discover a new direction. This can happen, however, through focusing not only on *what kind* of change Vatican II introduced, but also, perhaps even primarily, on *how* it was introduced. He proposes that the main change which was brought by Vatican II was a change in style, in the Church's manner of speaking. He lists many other dimensions which differentiate Vatican II from the previous twenty councils of the Church,[57] but he insists that the most crucial difference was the new way of speaking adopted by the Council. For O'Malley, as much as an ecclesial or historical event Vatican II was "a language-event."[58] He argues that "in speaking in a style different from previous councils, Vatican II in effect redefined the very nature of a council."[59] This, according to him, was the factor which changed the Catholic Church most and which made it possible to speak about "before" and "after Vatican II."[60]

2.2. A matter of style (language event)

The components and nuances of O'Malley's theory cannot be explained here in great detail; however, some of its main theses need to be explained.[61] O'Malley begins by recognising the general importance of the style in which a given message is conveyed. In general terms "a style choice is an identity choice, a personality choice." "The style is the man"; that is, the way we speak is inseparable from who we are.[62] In the case of the language adopted by the fathers of Vatican II, this choice has to do with "the kind of institution the council wanted the church to be."[63] The conciliar decision to adapt a manner of speaking different from the way the councils spoke before was "much more than a tactic or a strategy, much more than simply the adoption of a more 'pastoral language.'"[64] Such a change in language "indicated and induced a shift in values or priorities."[65] This is because "style is the ultimate expression of meaning. It does not adorn meaning but is meaning. It is a hermeneutical key par excellence,"[66] and any hermeneutics of Vatican II which does not take this into account will necessarily have to be incomplete and ultimately unsuccessful.

What exactly did Vatican II change in the Church's way of speaking? O'Malley argues that it "radically modified the legislative and judicial model that had prevailed since the first council, Nicea, in 325, that it virtually abandoned it."[67] He says that "in its place Vatican II put a model largely based on persuasion and invitation" and concludes that "this was a momentous shift."[68] The Council "largely abandoned the Scholastic framework that had dominated Catholic theology since the thirteenth century"[69] by replacing the legal mode of speaking ("do this, do not do that, or . . .") with a "rhetoric of invitation and dialogue."[70] This was done by abandoning some old words and expressions and introducing new ones unknown to conciliar language before. The most obvious linguistic absence in the conciliar texts is the decision to abstain from issuing canons. Canons had always been a standard way of defining those doctrines which were erroneous, and they would generally use the following formula: "If anyone should . . ., let him be anathema." Canons would be, as O'Malley explains, "as unambiguous as possible," and they would draw clear lines through speaking "a language that tried unmistakably to distinguish 'who's in' and 'who's out'" and would often also include penalties for not complying with the teaching (exclusion from the community of believers would be the most obvious one).[71] The adoption of such a rhetoric and of such an approach "clearly manifests the assumption that a council is a legislative-judicial body," and O'Malley recalls that "Vatican I, for instance, issued 18 canons, whereas Trent issued more than 130 for its doctrinal decrees alone and did much the same for its disciplinary enactments."[72] Vatican II, however, issued "no canons, no anathemas, no verdicts of 'guilty as charged'"[73] and "notably missing are words of alienation, exclusion, enmity, words of threat and intimidation, words of surveillance and punishment."[74] All this, however, does not mean the Council did not intend to teach. Although it did not define any new doctrine, at least not in a technical sense,[75] it did present teaching and did so at a length which greatly exceeded that of previous councils.[76] However, it moved away from the standard way of doing this and it introduced "a rhetoric of invitation and dialogue" which "encourage[s] conversion, an interior change that is induced by and then expressed by a new way of speaking and behaving."[77] It replaced the rhetoric of "lawmaker, police officer, or judge" with that of "guide, partner, friend, and inspired helpmate"[78] thanks to which the conciliar documents are "intent on winning inner assent to truths and values and on winning appreciation for them."[79] The documents, to a large extent, "engage in a rhetoric of praise and congratulation" through adoption of a style which is "less autocratic and more collaborative," "willing to listen to different viewpoints and take them into account," "open and aboveboard," "less unilateral in its decision-making," "committed to fair play and to working with persons and institutions outside the Catholic community," assuming "innocence until guilt is proven" and eschewing "secret oaths, anonymous denunciations, and inquisitorial tactics."[80]

This general shift in style detected by O'Malley is evident not only in the notable absence of canons and other standard conciliar expressions, but also in the eminent presence of certain expressions unknown to conciliar vocabulary before Vatican II. He groups the new vocabulary of the Council into categories: (1) "horizontal words" (these include expressions such as "people of God," "brothers and sisters," "the priesthood of all believers," "collegiality)"; (2) "words of reciprocity" ("cooperation," "partnership," "collaboration," "dialogue," "conversation"); (3) humility words ("church as pilgrim," or "servant," the term "presbyter" used to distinguish between ordained priesthood and the priesthood of all believers); (4) "change words" ("development," "progress," "evolution," *aggiornamento*); and (5) interiority words ("charisms," "joy and hope, grief and anguish," "conscience").[81] According to O'Malley, these words, unknown in previous conciliar documents, "cannot be considered casual asides or simple window-dressing-'mere rhetoric'" because "they are used far too insistently and too characteristically for that."[82] They "do not occur here and there but are an across-the-board phenomenon" and they "allow us to determine patterns that provide a horizon of interpretation."[83] They "express an overall orientation and a coherence in values and outlook that markedly contrast with those of previous councils and, indeed, with most official ecclesiastical documents up to that point" and "taken as a whole, they convey the sweep of a newly and forcefully specified style of the church."[84] The "panegyric-epideictic genre" adopted by the Council points towards reconciliation and persuasion and is present in all of the conciliar documents: "for the first time in history, a council would take care self-consciously to infuse its documents with vocabulary and themes that cut across them all."[85] Due to the presence of the new style "across the board," it is possible to talk about a certain orientation, a general direction to which the Council points. Thus, it is possible to define the "spirit of the Council" without divorcing it from the letter; in fact, the spirit is to be found in the letter, not only in what it says, but also in how it says it and what it decides not to say.

It is neither possible nor necessary to critically analyse O'Malley's thesis about Vatican II in this work. It will have to suffice to mention that, as with every other theological thesis, his ideas met with general acclaim and the endorsement of some scholars[86] and criticism of others.[87] What needs to be said is that the hermeneutics of the Council which focuses on the style of its documents, including their "deliberate ambiguities," genre and general orientation, is well known and often used as a justification for promoting the view of Vatican II as a "new opening" in the history of the Church. The Church was changed, and this change came about through language in which the magisterium of the Church chose to speak. In the following chapter it will be argued that such a hermeneutics can also be applied to interpretation of *AL*. In fact, on the day of the presentation of the document, certain hints regarding such hermeneutics were made by those who were charged with the task of introducing *AL* to the public. The subsequent history of the interpretation of the document suggests that this interpretation has indeed been adopted and that in the course of time it will remain the principal way of reading *AL*.

Notes

1 See Faggioli, "Vatican II: History and the Narratives," 762, who refers to Giuseppe Alberigo, *Transizione epocale: Studi sul concilio Vaticano II* (Bologna: Il Mulino, 2009), 29–45. See also Alberigo's "VIII: Transition to a New Age" in edited by him *History of Vatican II, Vol 5: The Council and the Transition: The Fourth Period and the End of the Council: September 1965–December 1965*, English version ed. Joseph A. Komonchak, trans. Matthew J. O'Connel (Maryknoll, NY: Orbis Books/Leuven: Peeters, 2006), 628. Alberigo's negative opinion about these compromises is quite clear: "[they] weakened the conceptual and programmatic force of some pages of Vatican II and, in the postconciliar period, provided the basis for recurring and barren debates. It was the very nature of this Council and its final texts that they limited the importance of compromises."
2 John O'Malley, "Developments, Reforms and Two Great Reformations: Towards a Historical Assessment of Vatican II," *Theological Studies* 44 (1983): 373–406, at 392 and 396.
3 John O'Malley, "Reform, Historical Consciousness, and Vatican II's *Aggiornamento*," *Theological Studies* 32 (1971): 573–601, at 574.
4 Herman J. Pottmeyer, "A New Phase in the Reception of Vatican II: Twenty Years of Interpretation of the Council," in *The Reception of Vatican II*, eds. Giuseppe Alberigo, Jean-Pierre Jossua and Joseph A. Komonchak (Washington, DC: Catholic University of America Press, 1987), 27–43, at 37.
5 Ormond Rush, *Still Interpreting Vatican II: Some Hermeneutical Principles* (New York: Paulist Press, 2004), 27.
6 Ibid., 27.
7 Otto Herman Pesch, *Das Zweite Vaticanische Konzil: Vorgeschichte – Verlauf – Ergebnisse – Nachgeschichte* (Würzburg: Echter Verlag, 2001), 150–154. The volume is now available in English as *The Second Vatican Council: Prehistory – Event – Results – Posthistory*, trans. Deirdre Dempsey (Milwaukee, WI: Marquette University Press 2014).
8 Rush, *Still Interpreting Vatican II*, 28. See also his "Toward a Comprehensive Interpretation of the Council and Its Documents," *Theological Studies* 73 (2012): 547–569, at 551 on deliberate juxtapositions and open-endedness of the documents and at 564–567 on the task of creative interpretation and ongoing reception ("hermeneutics of receivers").
9 Rush, *Still Interpreting Vatican II*, 29.
10 There is no shortage of works which even in their titles call Vatican II precisely that. See for example Lucien Richard, Daniel T. Harrington, and John W. O'Malley, eds., *Vatican II: The Unfinished Agenda: A Look to the Future* (New York: Paulist Press, 1987); Austen Ivereigh, ed., *Unfinished Journey: The Church 40 Years after Vatican II: Essays for John Wilkins* (New York/London: Continuum, 2003); Richard R. Gaillardetz, *An Unfinished Council: Vatican II, Pope Francis, and the Renewal of Catholicism* (Collegeville, MN: Liturgical Press, 2015); Paul Lakeland, *A Council That Will Never End: Lumen Gentium and the Church Today* (Collegeville, MN: Liturgical Press, 2013).

11 Rush, *Still Interpreting Vatican II*, 29.
12 Rush refers here to Louis Alonso Schökel and María Bravo, *A Manual of Hermeneutics*, trans. Brook W.R. Pearson (New York/Sheffield, UK: Sheffield Academic Press, 1998), 170; see Rush, *Still Interpreting Vatican II*, 69. Neil Ormerod, "Vatican II: Continuity or Discontinuity? Toward an Ontology of Meaning," *Theological Studies* 71 (2010): 609–636, at 635–636 makes a similar point when he writes that "the most that the council could do was authorise the beginnings of a process whose end point is not yet in sight."
13 Joseph Ratzinger, "VII: Fortieth Anniversary of the Constitution on the Sacred Liturgy: A Look Back and a Look Forward," in Joseph Ratzinger, *Theology of the Liturgy: The Sacramental Foundation of Christian Existence*, ed. Michael J. Miller, trans. Kenneth Baker, S.J. and Henry Taylor, et al. (San Francisco: Ignatius Press, 2014): 574–588, at 575. *SC* is not the only document of the Council where Ratzinger admits a tension, even a contradiction. Regarding *Lumen Gentium* he talks about "constant tension between full papal power and full collegial power" which reflects "the internal struggle of the Council and the difficulty of arriving at a statement encompassing the whole complexity of history. Whenever one pole is mentioned, this is immediately counteracted by the balancing mention of the other pole." See his *Theological Highlights of Vatican II* (New York/Mahwah, NJ: Paulist Press, 2009, reprinted from 1966), 166. Regarding *Dignitatis Humanae*, he considers the attempt to harmonise the traditional approach declared in paragraph 1 with the new one as unsuccessful, because what one finds in the later part of the text is "something new, something that is quite different from what was found, for example, in the statements of Pius XI and Pius XII." He concludes that "it would have been better to omit these compromising formulas or to reformulate them in line with the later text," see *Theological Highlights of Vatican II*, 212. Ratzinger's critical evaluation of *GS*, including the document's vagueness and open-ended character, deserves a more lengthy treatment, such as the one carried out by Tracey Rowland, *Ratzinger's Faith: The Theology of Pope Benedict XVI* (Oxford: University Press, 2008), Chapter II: "*Gaudium et Spes* and the Importance of Christ," 30–47. For more on this see also Avery Dulles, "From Ratzinger to Benedict," *First Things* 160 (February 2006): 24–29.
14 Richard R. Gaillardetz, *The Church in the Making: Lumen Gentium, Christus Dominus, Orientalium Ecclesiarum* (New York/Mahwah: Paulist Press, 2006), xvii–xviii.
15 Kasper, *Theology and Church*, 170.
16 O'Malley, "Development, Reforms, and Two Great Reformations," 398.
17 Ibid., 398.
18 Quoted in Marchetto, *The Second Vatican Ecumenical Council*, 671.
19 Ibid. where Marchetto's critical commentary of this view can also be found. Marchetto's critique is endorsed by Matthew L. Lamb and Matthew Levering, "Introduction" in edited by them *Vatican II: Renewal within Tradition* (New York: Oxford University Press, 2008), 3–22, at 7 where the authors complain that the texts of the Council are too often "approached as products of power struggles between the liberals and the conservatives, with one side winning this passage and the other side winning that." Such an interpretation should, in their view, give way to "what Pope Benedict XVI calls a hermeneutics of

reform in continuity with the two millennial traditions of Catholic thought and wisdom."

20 Tagle, 450 and 452 of *History of Vatican II*. Every history of Vatican II includes some reference to the "Black Week," the week of the third session, when Pope Paul VI intervened very directly in the conciliar process through (1) postponing the voting on the document on religious liberty, (2) introducing some changes into the document on ecumenism, (3) adding the "Preliminary Explanatory Note" to the Dogmatic Constitution on the Church and (4) proclaiming Mary as Mother of the Church. The given author's approach to that week often illustrates their theological position regarding the interpretation of the Council as a whole. For example, Marchetto questions the whole idea of the existence of "Black Week," or at least the negative expression used to describe it, and argues that "the week in question was actually a week when many things got clarified" (*The Second Vatican Council*, 684). On the other side of the spectrum, Thomas Hughson goes as far as to ask how it is possible that events such as the Black Week "did not render the proceedings [of the Council] impervious to the Spirit"? See his "Interpreting Vatican II: 'A New Pentecost'," *Theological Studies* 69 (2008): 3–37, at 36–37.

21 Ibid.

22 Alessandro Rovati, "Mercy Is a Person: Pope Francis and the Christological Turn in Moral Theology," *Journal of Moral Theology* 6/2 (2017): 48–69, at 55.

23 George Lindbeck, *The Future of Roman Catholic Theology: Vatican II – Catalyst for Change* (Philadelphia: Fortress, 1970).

24 B. C. Butler, "Forward" in Lindbeck, *The Future of Roman Catholic Theology*, ix.

25 Lindbeck, *The Future of Roman Catholic Theology*, 3.

26 Ibid., 3.

27 Avery Dulles, "Vatican II: The Myth and the Reality," *America* (24 February 2003): 7–11, at 7.

28 Lindbeck, *The Future of Roman Catholic Theology*, 4. He develops these ideas in "A Protestant Point of View," in *Vatican II: An Interfaith Appraisal*, ed. John H. Miller, C.S.C. (Notre Dame, IN: University of Notre Dame Press, 1996), 219–230.

29 Antonio Ascerbi, "Receiving Vatican II in a Changes Historical Context," *Concilium* 146 (1981): 77–84, at 77 and 81. The author also gives the post-conciliar liturgical reform as an example of "interpretation that remained faithful to the Council by going beyond the letter of the Council," see 81.

30 Kasper, *Theology and Church*, 176.

31 Rush, *Still Interpreting Vatican II*, 80.

32 Ibid., 34.

33 Ibid., 55.

34 Ibid. One could wonder whether O'Malley's warnings about the danger of manipulation of the documents of Vatican II (see previous pages) would not somehow apply to this interpretation, especially if it lacks some precise criteria for such a "creative interpretation." Absence of such criteria might mean that in practice anything could be attributed to Vatican II in the name of this kind of creativity.

35 Rush, *Still Interpreting Vatican II*, *passim*.

36 Massimo Faggioli, *A Council for the Global Church: Receiving Vatican II in History* (Augsburg, MN: Fortress Press, 2015), 334–335.

37 O'Malley, *What Happened at Vatican II*, 3.

38 Ibid., 12.
39 Giuseppe Dossetti, "Per una valutazione globale del magistero del Vaticano II," in *Il Vaticano II: Frammenti di una riflessione*, ed. F. Margiotta Broglio (Bologna: Il Mulino, 1996), 24–25, 101, cited in Alberigo, *History of Vatican II*, 627.
40 Ibid.
41 Romano Amerio, *Iota Unum: A Study of Change in the Catholic Church in the Twentieth Century*, trans. John P. Parson (Kansas City, MO: Sarto House, 1996), 99, quoted in Faggioli, *Vatican II: The Battle for Meaning*, 27.
42 Michael Davies, *Liturgical Time Bombs in Vatican II: Destruction of the Faith through Changes in Catholic Worship* (Charlotte, NC: Tan Books, 2003).
43 Rush, *Still Interpreting Vatican II*, 29: "The 'spirit' of the Council was to leave seemingly contradictory positions deliberately side by side."
44 "The theological interpretation of the conciliar doctrine must consider all the documents both in themselves and in their close interrelationship, so that the integral meaning of the Council's affirmations – often very complex – might be understood and expressed." Synod of Bishops of 1985, "Final Report," *Origins* 15 (1985): 445–446.
45 Rush, *Still Interpreting Vatican II*, 41.
46 Massimo Faggioli, "Quaestio Disputata: *Sacrosanctum Concilium* and the Meaning of Vatican II," *Theological Studies* 71 (2010): 437–452, at 437.
47 John O'Malley, *What Happened at Vatican II* (Cambridge, MA/London: Harvard University Press, 2010), 3.
48 John O'Malley, "Misdirections: The Sure-Fire Ways to Mix Up the Teaching of Vatican II," *America* (4 February 2015): 25–27, at 26. See also his "'The Hermeneutic of Reform': A Historical Analysis," *Theological Studies* 73 (2012): 517–546, at 541.
49 Gilles Routhier, "Vatican II: Relevance and Future," *Theological Studies* 74 (2013): 537–554, at 541.
50 Routhier, "Vatican II: Relevance and Future," 541.
51 Rush, *Still Interpreting Vatican II*, 40–48.
52 Joseph A. Komonchak lists at least three different definitions: (1) the "spirit of renewal and reform that the calling of the council evoked and that the texts of Vatican II were meant to embody and articulate"; (2) "spirit that is thought to have been at work in the conciliar process and to have provided its distinctive character, which, if it was indeed embodied and articulated in the final texts, cannot be reduced to what they say"; and (3) "what 'Vatican II' would have said and done if no conservatives had been present in Rome during those years and the spirit of renewal and reform had not been forced into channels too narrow for its full flood into the life of the church," see Joseph A. Komonchak, "Benedict XVI and the Interpretation of Vatican II," in *The Crisis of Authority in Catholic Modernity*, eds. Michael J. Lacy and Francis Oakley (New York: Oxford Press, 2011), 93–110, at 106–107.
53 O'Malley, *What Happened at Vatican II*, 11.
54 Ibid., 52.
55 In his opinion these are the question of change in the Church's teaching and practice, the question of the relationship between the centre of the Church and periphery and the style and model of authority and its exercise. See *What Happened at Vatican II*, 12.
56 Ibid., 12.

57 John O'Malley, "Vatican II: Did Anything Happen?," *Theological Studies* 67 (2006): 3–33, at 11–12 he lists the following: an unprecedented number of bishops taking part (approx. 2500) from an incomparable number of countries (116), official recognition and influence of theologians who, a few years before the Council, had their orthodoxy questioned by the Holy Office, presence of non-Catholic observers and their indirect influence through interactions outside the official sessions, mass media's powerful presence and coverage, the fact that the Council addressed the whole Church (not only the clergy) or even "all humanity" (*GS*) on various subjects never before discussed at a council (war, peace, poverty, family, etc.) and an unprecedented number of documents produced (16).
58 John O'Malley, "Vatican II: Official Norms," *America* (31 March 2003): 11–14, at 14; O'Malley, *What Happened at Vatican II*, 306.
59 O'Malley, "Vatican II: Official Norms," 14.
60 O'Malley, "Vatican II: Did Anything Happen?," 32–33.
61 A fine treatment of his thought, including the historical process of development in it, can be found in Ann M. C. Nolan, "Vatican II: Changing the Style of Being Church," *Australasian Catholic Record* 98/4 (October 2012): 397–407.
62 John O'Malley, "The Style of Vatican II," *America* (24 February 2003): 12–15, *passim*.
63 O'Malley, *What Happened at Vatican II*, 305.
64 Ibid., 12.
65 Ibid.
66 Ibid., 49.
67 Ibid., 11.
68 Ibid.
69 Ibid., 46.
70 Ibid., 47–48.
71 O'Malley, "Vatican II: Did Anything Happen?," 19.
72 Ibid., 19.
73 O'Malley, *What Happened at Vatican II*, 45. This is all the more remarkable since "the Roman Synod of 1960, the purported 'dress rehearsal' for Vatican II, issued 773 canons," see O'Malley, "'The Hermeneutic of Reform'," 542.
74 O'Malley, "Vatican II: Did Anything Happen?," 27.
75 This is in line with Pope John XXIII's explanation that "the salient point of this Council is not, therefore, a discussion of one article or another of the fundamental doctrine of the Church which has repeatedly been taught by the Fathers and by ancient and modern theologians, and which is presumed to be well known and familiar to all." See "Pope John's Opening Speech to the Council, [Gaudet Mater Ecclesia]," in *The Documents of Vatican II*, ed. Walter M. Abbott (New York: America Press, 1966), 710–719, at 715.
76 O'Malley, "Vatican II: Did Anything Happen?," 10 states that the pagination of the sixteen documents produced by Vatican II is "almost twice the length of the decrees of Trent, and the decrees of Trent and Vatican II together equal in volume the decrees of all the other 19 councils taken together."
77 O'Malley, *What Happened at Vatican II*, 47–48.
78 O'Malley, "Vatican II: Did Anything Happen?," 31.
79 O'Malley, *What Happened at Vatican II*, 306.
80 O'Malley, "Vatican II: Did Anything Happen?," 31.
81 O'Malley, *What Happened at Vatican II*, 49–50.

82 Ibid., 49.
83 Ibid.
84 Ibid., 306–307. Stephen Schloesser, "Against Forgetting: Memory, History, Vatican II," *Theological Studies* 67 (2006): 275–319 analyses the moral dimensions of changes introduced (and initiated) at Vatican II and calls the conciliar language "a literary genre with a sharp ethical edge" (297).
85 O'Malley, *What Happened at Vatican II*, 310.
86 These include Faggioli, *Vatican II: The Battle for Meaning*, 117, 130; Rush, *Still Interpreting Vatican II*, 37–39, Ormerod, "Vatican II: Continuity or Discontinuity?," 634; Schloesser, "Against Forgetting: Memory, History, Vatican II," 277–279.
87 These include Avery Dulles, "Vatican II: Substantive Teaching: A Reply to John W. O'Malley and Others," *America* (31 March 2003): 14–17; Kenneth Whitehead, "Vatican II Then and Now: A Review Essay on John O'Malley, S.J.'s *What Happened at Vatican II*," *Nova et Vetera*, English Edition 8/2 (2010): 467–483.

3 *Amoris Laetita* and the "spirit of Vatican II"

In this chapter certain general similarities between the texts of the Second Vatican Council and *AL* will be identified and explained. An argument will be made that the "the spirit of Vatican II" is present in *AL* not only in the "attitude of listening" (Tagle and Forte), but also in those two features of its text which were identified in the previous chapter, that is, in the existence of "deliberate ambiguities" which can interpreted as new openings, and in the adoption of a new style of speaking.

3.1. Ambiguities in the texts – towards "creative fidelity"

As discussed, many of the scholars who acknowledge the existence of difficulties in interpreting Vatican II due to ambiguities contained in its texts believe that the most accurate hermeneutics of the Council would be the one which gives most consideration to the impulses towards the new contained in them. These impulses should be interpreted not as the last word on the matter, but as a stimulus for further developments. As Joseph Ratzinger stated in 1966, "the texts of a Council are not meant to save work for theologians," but "should stimulate such work and open new horizons" since the documents are "not a prize to be confidently carried off" but can only serve as a beginning.[1] Furthermore, attention must be paid not only to *what* the texts say, but also to *how* they say it, since "almost more important than the solutions offered by the text is the attitude behind the text, which discovered here a new way of speaking."[2]

How can these two hermeneutical principles be helpful for interpreting *AL*? Similarly to documents of Vatican II, *AL* is a document which in many respects is profound, inspiring and moving, but at the same time it is also unclear, ambiguous and full of difficult compromises. In fact, it is most ambiguous in those passages which were most anticipated by many – that is, in the treatment of the topic of pastoral practices towards those Catholics who live in irregular unions, especially those who are divorced and civilly remarried (Chapter VIII). Those who wish to emphasise the continuity of the document with the previous magisterial teaching will find in *AL* passages which very strongly confirm the traditional Catholic teaching on such issues as the indissolubility of marriage (nos. 52–53, 62, 77, 86, 123–124, 134, 178, 243), same-sex unions (251), birth control (68, 80), the "ideology of gender" (56) or reproductive technologies (56).[3] Others, however, stress that apart from obvious continuities with the previous teachings and policies, there are also certain discontinuities. Vatican II quoted the previous two councils (Vatican I and Trent) and recent popes (especially Pius XII) extensively, yet it also introduced something profoundly new. Francis also quotes John Paul II and Benedict XVI, but at the same time he does not just repeat what they said but brings in elements of novelty. He does this in the same two ways of Vatican II: first, through juxtaposing the old, traditional teaching and practices with the new; and second, through a change in rhetoric.

The issue which became most debated in the aftermath of the publication of *AL* was, as expected, the possibility of divorced and civilly remarried Catholics to receive the sacraments of Penance and Eucharist. At times various observers (mainly non-theologians) oversimplify the matter by posing the question of whether their admission to these sacraments is possible now, after *AL*. If the question is posed this way, it leads to some misunderstandings since it implicitly suggests that it was not possible before *AL*. For the sake of precision it needs to be clarified that the issue here is not really *if* but *how* those Catholics who live in non-sacramental second unions can partake in the sacraments. John Paul II in his 1981 post-synodal apostolic exhortation *Familiaris Consortio* (*FC*)[4] envisaged this possibility under the condition of living "as brother and sister" (*FC* 84).[5] The real question is, therefore, not whether *AL* makes the admission of these people to the Eucharist possible, but whether it waives the conditions set out by John Paul II. Is the requirement of living in continence still absolute, as set out by John Paul II, or is it not absolute anymore and, thus, are exceptions possible?

Some commentators argue that after *AL* the conditions of John Paul II still stand, some deem that they do not, while others limit themselves to stating that the document is not clear on this. Adam G. Cooper states that "almost any 'party' within and beyond the Church can no doubt find in it a grab-bag of quotes to further whatever agenda it wishes to pursue."[6] Similarly, Carl Olsen asserts that "this is a text that has something for everyone, and a text that will likely frustrate everyone as well,"[7] and William L. Portier warns that *AL* is "bound to disappoint a wide range of readers."[8] Nicholas Austin argues that "[a]nyone looking for a 'progressive' or 'liberal' pope will feel as let down as those hoping for a straightforward reaffirmation of the status quo,"[9] while Thomas Knieps-Port le Roi and Roger Burggraeve opine that "the pope has managed to remain faithful to the church's tradition and teaching while at the same time turning it upside down."[10] The document does not clearly state anywhere that it lifts the condition set out by John Paul II, but neither does it repeat it. The exhortation does refer to John Paul II almost fifty times, and even references *FC* 84, but it does not repeat the condition of continence as a necessary requirement (it only mentions it as a "possibility," as discussed later). If O'Malley is correct in stating that what is *not* being said is as important as what *is* being said, then this might be one of the most noteworthy absences in the document. While some interpret it as not upholding the rule anymore ("if the Pope wanted to uphold it he would have said it"), others interpret it as the opposite ("if the Pope wanted to change such an important rule he would have said it").[11] As Leroy Huizenga observed, "[s]ome will see in the several references to *Familiaris Consortio* a ringing endorsement of a conservative read of Pope John Paul II's magisterium, or hear in the sound of silence tacit approval to move forward in new directions."[12]

Francis quotes *FC* 84 when he talks about couples who "for serious reasons, such as the children's upbringing . . . cannot satisfy the obligation to separate."[13] Yet he does not quote the condition of living in continence in the body of the text, but instead gives a footnote in which he states:

> In such situations, many people, knowing and accepting the possibility of living "as brothers and sisters" which the Church offers them, point out that if certain expressions of intimacy are lacking, "it often happens that faithfulness is endangered and the good of the children suffers."[14]

The Pope then gives reference to Vatican II's *GS* 51, which states that "where the intimacy of married life is broken off, its faithfulness can sometimes be imperilled and its quality of fruitfulness ruined, for then the upbringing of the children and the courage to accept new ones are both endangered."[15] Does recognising this difficulty mean that there are cases when meeting the condition of continence is not possible due to higher priorities (such as keeping the new family together) and that in these cases the condition of continence is not absolute? Or does it simply mean that the Pope recognises how difficult it might be to find a solution in a given particular situation of a family, however, falls short of stating that sometimes sexual relations outside a valid, sacramental marriage are not sinful? What is the purpose of this footnote? It is hard to know and, thus, the text provokes conflicting interpretations. Gerald O'Collins, for example, reads in it that Francis does not endorse this solution and that he "leaves it behind,"[16] and Martin M. Lintner considers any other position than this to be unreasonable.[17] Nicholas Austin believes that while "Francis is not giving a blanket permission," it could be "one of those cases in which mercy, discerning what is possible 'for now', might indicate a different route for pastoral advice than the traditional *frater-soror* solution,"[18] and Basilio Petrà opines that confessors are not absolutely obligated by the norm of *FC* 84 anymore.[19] Stephan Kampowski, on the other hand, argues that the Pope's intention was simply "to find a merciful tone and show awareness of sociological and statistical realities," without, however, changing the traditional teaching or practice.[20] Olson considers using this conciliar quote (*GS* 51) "as an argument for divorced and 'remarried' couples to have sexual relations" as "misleading and troubling,"[21] while Edward Peters thinks linking the situation of "married couples observing periodic abstinence" with "the angst public adulterers experience when they cease in engaging in illicit sexual intercourse" is a serious misuse of conciliar teaching by the Pope.[22]

At another point, Francis states:

> Because of forms of conditioning and mitigating factors, it is possible that in an objective situation of sin – which may not be subjectively culpable, or fully such – a person can be living in God's grace, can love and can also grow in the life of grace and charity, while receiving the Church's help to this end.[23]

He then attaches a footnote (n. 351) to this sentence which has been described as "the most famous footnote in the history of the Church"[24] or at least in her contemporary history.[25] The footnote states that "in certain cases, this can include the help of the sacraments." The Pope does not specify which sacraments he means, but this statement is followed by two quotations from his apostolic exhortation *Evangelii Gaudium* (*EG*),[26] one about Penance ("the confessional must not be a torture chamber, but rather an encounter with the Lord's mercy" – no. 44) and Eucharist (it is "not a prize for the perfect, but a powerful medicine and nourishment for the weak" – no. 47). How is this statement exactly to be interpreted? Is Pope Francis in this footnote waiving John Paul II's condition? The matter remains divisive both in terms of content (was there a change?) and its form (can such a significant change be introduced in this way, i.e. in an unclear footnote?).

Edward Peters argues that *AL* does not license the change of policy laid out by John Paul II and states that "if Francis had wanted to authorise the administration of holy Communion to divorced-and-remarried Catholics (and he did not want to repudiate CCC 2384, 1650, etc.) he would have *had* to have wrought a change in the law contained in Canon 915 [of the Canon Law]"[27] (emphasis original), which states that "those who have been excommunicated or interdicted after the imposition or declaration of the penalty and others obstinately persevering in manifest grave sin are not to be admitted to holy communion."[28] He concludes that since *AL* "is not a legislative document, it contains no legislative or authentic interpretative language and it does not discuss Canon 915," and thus "those who think *Amoris* has cleared the path to the Communion rail for Catholics in irregular marriages are hearing words that the pope (whatever might be his personal inclinations) simply did not say."[29] Livio Melina is also of the opinion that the only one possible conclusion from reading Chapter 8 of *AL* is that "*AL* does not change the Church's discipline."[30] Austin believes that "Francis stops short of positively affirming that reception of communion for the civilly remarried is acceptable; yet . . . he leaves it open as a possibility *in certain cases*."[31] With the passage of time and with certain recent interventions of Pope Francis (see later), the growing majority of commentators, however, tend to agree that this particular passage from *AL* legitimises exceptions from the general rule and the conditions attached to it by *FC* 84.[32]

Cardinal Christoph Schönborn, who was charged by Pope Francis with the task of presenting *AL* to the public on a press conference on 8 April 2016 and who the Pope considers to be the ultimate interpreter of the document,[33] when asked about why would such an important change in the Church's policy be placed in a footnote rather than explained clearly in the body of the text, answered that in his opinion the reason for placing this phrase in a footnote has a symbolic meaning, that is, that it should not be the centre of our attention. This is because the Pope does not want the readers to focus only on this particular issue and prefers them to keep the big picture in sight at all times.[34]

Confusion regarding the meaning of this and other passages of the document inspired cardinals Carlo Caffarra, Joachim Meisner, Walter Brandmüller and Raymond Leo Burke to seek clarification from the Pope regarding not only the alleged change of sacramental discipline concerning pastoral care of divorced and civilly remarried, but also regarding some fundamental principles of Catholic moral theology presented in John Paul II's encyclical letter *Veritatis Splendor* from 1993.[35] Their "five *dubia*" (doubts) were sent to the Pope privately; however, having received no response, the cardinals decided to make them public.[36] The *dubia* have not been answered by Francis to date, and some argue that it is unlikely that they will be answered in any way.[37] Cardinal Gerhard Müller, while serving as prefect for the Congregation for the Doctrine of the Faith (his five-year tenure was completed in July 2017 and Francis, in an unprecedented move, decided to not extend it, despite Müller's relatively young age), expressed publicly his opinion that the practice of the Church regarding divorced and remarried was not, indeed could not, be changed by Francis and that the condition of *FC* 84 still stands and always will.[38] The Congregation itself, however, did not issue any official document about this. On the other hand, Cardinal

Francesco Coccopalmerio, president of the Pontifical Council for Legislative Texts, issued a booklet in which he states that while the condition of continence remains the preferred option, in some cases it might not be absolute.[39]

The most explicit statements about this issue which Francis himself has made to date are (1) his response to a journalist question at a press conference on the occasion of his return from his trip to Lesvos on 16 April 2016,[40] and (2) his endorsement of the guidelines which bishops of Buenos Aires issued for their Pastoral Region. These guidelines state that in some cases it is possible to admit individual divorced and remarried Catholics to the sacraments of Penance and Eucharist without the absolute condition of living in continence (although living "as brother and sister" is presented as a preferable option). The Pope's letter was a private response to a request for approval of the Argentinian bishops' guidelines regarding the interpretation of Chapter VIII, and in it Francis confirmed that "there are no other interpretations" of *AL*, that their document was very good and that it completely explained the meaning of Chapter VIII of *AL*. This private correspondence was leaked to the public and soon after it questions arose about both its authenticity and its magisterial status. With regard to concerns about authenticity, it was shortly confirmed by *L'Osservatore Romano*[41] and by the Vatican Radio[42] that the document was authentic. With regard to its magisterial status, the Pope's letter was subsequently placed at the official Vatican web page[43] and finally published in *Acta Apostolicae Saedis* (*AAS*)[44] which, as the Code of Canon Law states, is "the official commentary of the Holy See where universal ecclesiastical laws are promulgated.[45] Additionally, Cardinal Pietro Parolin, Secretary of State, attached a note to this publication in *AAS* in which he states that Francis decreed that the two documents (Buenos Aires bishops' guidelines and his endorsement) be published both at the Vatican web page and in *AAS* as "authentic magisterium."[46] This was welcomed by many as the end of the ongoing controversy and as an official declaration of how at least certain ambiguous passages from *AL* should be interpreted. However, some commentators still remain unconvinced about the magisterial status of the Pope's endorsement.[47]

In the aftermath of the publication of *AL*, a number of commentators stated that it is not easy to interpret the Pope's words contained in Chapter 8 of the document (see previous paragraphs). However, this fact alone is a significant development which should not be overlooked. The ambiguous language of *AL* is intriguing when compared to the language of Francis' predecessors (John Paul II and Benedict XVI) who tended to write with a marked clarity. Many theologians agreed with the content of what they were saying and many did not; some found their reasoning convincing, others found it lacking; however, there were not too many disputes about what the given pope was actually saying. With the pontificate of Francis, this is changing. With his "pastoral language," homilies delivered off the cuff, unauthorised interviews, press conferences in airplanes, private conversations and famous private phone calls we have perhaps entered a new way of exercising papal magisterium. In fact, what we are experiencing now might be more than just a different way of exercising the teaching office, but some form of redefinition of what the magisterium of the Bishop of Rome really is. This is an argument of Richard Gaillardetz who talks about a "pastoral magisterium" of Francis which "does not claim to have all the answers, nor does it provide definitive solutions to every controverted issue" but which, while acknowledging the normative character of current church teaching, "keeps open the possibility of further insight." This magisterium is "committed to cultivating an ecclesial atmosphere in which controverted questions can be freely debated, new insights can emerge, and the Spirit can work through the shared discernment of the *whole* people of God" (emphasis original).[48] Arnaud Join-Lambert agrees that Francis as "the Pope has abandoned the classical construction of texts by the magisterium – proceeding from the doctrinal to the pastoral" and admits that this has "destabilised some theologians and pastors."[49] And as William L. Portier explains,

> Francis's primary concern is neither doctrine nor theology. Rather, he's trying to start a pastoral revolution among the bishops, clergy, and people of the Catholic Church. If his two papal predecessors were about clarity and definition in tumultuous times, Francis wants to send missionary disciples out beyond the church's boundaries, clearly marked out over the past thirty-five years, to ecclesial peripheries where those in difficult marriage situations live.[50]

Moving away from "doctrinal" to "pastoral" language during the pontificate of Francis resembles the shift from allegedly legalistic and cold language of the first twenty councils of the Church to the "pastoral language" of Vatican II. Also, the ambiguous and open-ended character of certain texts of Vatican II comes to mind when reading *AL*. Just as in the conciliar texts, in *AL* one can find many traditional, reassuring statements which suggest to the conservative reader that no revolution is taking place here. At the same time, one can find certain new openings which suggest to a more progressive reader that something important has happened. Instead of being the last word on the matter, *AL* seeks to stimulate further development. Rather than clearly prescribing new regulations, Francis has chosen to open the door for possibilities which have not existed before and simply leave it there, without clearly stating the last word. Reading *AL* requires, thus, "creative fidelity," which was also required for reading the texts of Vatican II.

Francis seems to tolerate diverse interpretations of his document, which seems to be consistent with his principle of "sound 'decentralisation'" (*EG* 16). In *AL* 3 he states that "not all discussions of doctrinal, moral or pastoral issues need to be settled by interventions of the magisterium" and that "each country or region, moreover, can seek solutions better suited to its culture and sensitive to its traditions and local needs," which Christopher Lamb calls "arguably . . . the most important line" of the document.[51] Francis' decision to not answer the "five *dubia*," his emphasis on the need to avoid thinking in black-and-white categories,[52] his tolerance regarding diverse interpretations and implementation of *AL* (despite stating his own preference) seem to suggest that "creative fidelity" in application of his open-ended document is something that he expects and welcomes. Just like the ambiguous language of Vatican II opened the door to "creative fidelity" in its interpretation and facilitated the reforms which took place in the Church in the post-conciliar era, the ambiguous language of *AL* and its creative interpretation begin play the same role.

3.2. A matter of style (language event)

Apart from an open-ended language which juxtaposes traditional and innovative statements and allows for "creative interpretation" through focusing on the impulses to the new, "the spirit of Vatican II" was said to be present in the genre of the language of the Council (O'Malley). Can a change of rhetoric similar to that which took place in the documents of Vatican II be observed in *AL*?

Cardinal Schönborn in his presentation of *AL* called it "first and foremost, a 'linguistic event.'"[53] He said that in his opinion "something has changed in ecclesial discourse" and that this change, which was already taking place during the synods, consists of adopting a tone which is "richer in esteem, as if the different situations in life had simply been accepted, without being immediately judged or condemned."[54] This change of tone, which is continued in *AL*, is a reflection of "profound respect when faced with every person who is never firstly a 'problematic case' in a 'category', but rather a unique person, with his story and his journey with and towards God." In Schönborn's opinion, Francis continues on the path which he already indicated in *EG*, a path which, through adopting a new language, helps the Church to realise that we "must take off our shoes before the sacred ground of others."[55] The Pope speaks about all situations "without cataloguing them, without categorising," and his language is that of "invitation" and "encouragement" because he is "convinced that the Christian vision of marriage and the family . . . has an unchanged force of attraction."[56] Knieps-Port le

Roi and Burggraeve speak in a similar tone and argue that the document "does not rise the moral forefinger, does not condemn or prohibit any moral or pastoral practice, nor does it offer overly abstract or highly idealistic reflections."[57] On the contrary, the "gentle, warm and welcoming tone" reveals "a much more radical shift in the pope's theological approach to marriage and family."[58]

Is it possible to point to exact shifts in language which are present in *AL*, as O'Malley did with the documents of Vatican II? Schönborn himself points to two words which he considers to be the key to the whole document: "discernment" and "accompaniment." The word "discernment" (or "to discern") appears in the document thirty-six times (excluding headings).[59] "Accompaniment" (or "to accompany") in relation those living in irregular situations appears thirteen times (excluding headings). Francis himself, in his letter to Sergío Alfredo Fenoy, delegate of the Buenos Aires Pastoral Region, adds another two key words of the document: "welcome" (at least eight times used in this context) and "integration" (at least four times in this context).[60] Nicholas Austin talks about "Francis' Triptych" of "discernment," "gradualness" (gradual-related words occur ten times in the document) and "mercy" (more than thirty times),[61] and Cardinal Reinhard Marx points to "accompanying, discerning and integrating" as "the *cantus firmus*" on which every pastoral work based on *AL* must be built.[62] For sure, these expressions have been present in the magisterial documents before *AL*, but not in such great proportions and not as *the* key to unlocking the meaning of the given document.

The word "conscience" occurs in the document fourteen times. Again, it is certainly not a new word in the magisterium's vocabulary, but there are certain emphases in Francis' use of it which stand in tension with how previous popes used it. While in the writings of John Paul II one can find numerous instances of insisting on the need to understand conscience in the light of unchangeable norms derived from objective morality, Francis complains that this constant emphasis on the need to follow the objective moral norms presented by the magisterium leads to situations where pastors often "find it hard to make room for the consciences of the faithful, who very often respond as best they can to the Gospel amid their limitations, and are capable of carrying out their own discernment in complex situations."[63] While Francis does mention the need to form the conscience in accordance with objective moral norms (*AL* 222), he also states that

> conscience can do more than recognize that a given situation does not correspond objectively to the overall demands of the Gospel. It can also recognize with sincerity and honesty what for now is the most generous response which can be given to God, and come to see with a certain

moral security that it is what God himself is asking amid the concrete complexity of one's limits, while yet not fully the objective ideal.[64]

While Francis discusses the importance of conscience in the context of birth control twice (42 and 222), more frequently conscience is mentioned in the context of divorced Catholics living in second unions (265, 298, 300, 302, 303). One of the more famous sentences of the document reads: "We have been called to form consciences, not to replace them."[65]

John Finnis and Germain Grisez note that the word "adultery" occurs in the document only three times and always in the context of Jn 8:1–11 (the woman caught in adultery), never in the context of the divorced and remarried. They are also concerned that the expression "mortal sin" is absent from *AL*[66] and that "the indissolubility of marriage is never mentioned in *AL* 291–312, the paragraphs from which that Exhortation's directives about how to deal with the divorced and civilly remarried must be gathered."[67]

Tracey Rowland also notices a linguistic change of moving from describing the situation of those who live in second unions as "morally disordered" or "mortally sinful" to "irregular situations." Related to this is Cardinal Schönborn's emphasis that the Pope frequently uses inverted commas with the phrase "irregular situations" in the document.[68] Schönborn praises this measure because according to him it overcomes the distinction between "regular" and "irregular," which he considers to be artificial.[69] However, Rowland seems to not share Schönborn's enthusiasm about this change and fears that "chapter 8 gives the impression that the role of the Church as 'teacher of the Truth" and 'guardian of the deposit of the faith' should be muted so as to not scare people away from the Church." She thinks that phasing out such words as "disordered" or "sinful" and replacing them with "irregular" "is symptomatic of this muting."[70] Similarly, Branislav Kuljovsky complains that "*AL* never states that to knowingly and wilfully engage in non-marital sexual actions is always morally evil regardless of one's circumstances or motivations." He fears that portraying such way of behaving as "irregular," "incomplete," non-"ideal," "imperfect," or non-"full" "implies that one cannot evaluate such actions morally evil *per se*" and that "*AL*'s opting for such language undermines the existing teaching of the church on the moral absolutes."[71]

Todd A. Salzman and Michael G. Lawler point to the absence of the notion of *debitum obsequium* or *religiosum obsequium* (loyal or religious "respect" or "submission" to the teachings of the magisterium) in *AL*. They think that this absence is cause by Francis' preference for a subjective-oriented rather than objective-oriented understanding of conscience.[72]

The word "rule" appears thirteen times and usually has negative connotations – Francis acknowledges the importance of the existence of general or straightforward rules, but nearly every time he uses the word, he does it in order to emphasise that applying them always and everywhere to all situations is not possible and should be avoided.[73]

An important word which recurs in the document with a frequency previously unknown in magisterial documents is "ideal." It occurs twenty-two times in *AL* and is often presented as the aim for which all couples should strive, but which is often not immediately attainable. As a counterbalance to the "ideal," the word "concrete" appears at least twenty times in the document. The words "complex" or "complexity" appear sixteen times and the words "weak" or "weakness," used in the context of human inability to live up to proclaimed ideals, around fifteen times. The notion of human "limits" or "limitations" appears more than twenty times. Francis argues that while the Church can never fail to proclaim its full teaching vision of marriage and family (the ideal), she should also remain compassionate, understanding and willing to accompany those who do not live up to it (the concrete). Just as the documents of Vatican II in their panegyric style offer "an idealized portrait in order to excite admiration and appropriation,"[74] Francis presents a positive vision of the Christian family in the hope that its appeal will draw the readers to try to follow it. While Margaret Hickey notes that there is a change in approach here, "from one that demands to one that invites,"[75] Christian Brugger is worried that this emphasis might cause the reader to think that "the command of Christ is *merely* an ideal" (emphasis original).[76] He is concerned that while *AL* does state that this ideal should be proposed by the pastors, it also suggests that it cannot be presented as "a concrete command of God for everyone."[77]

The relationship between the ideal and the real in *AL* is one of the most evident linguistic shifts from previous magisterial documents. In *VS* John Paul II warned that "it would be a very serious error to conclude . . . that the Church's teaching is essentially only an 'ideal' which must then be adapted, proportioned, graduated to the so-called concrete possibilities of man" and insisted on the need to distinguish what kind of "man" are we talking about here: man "*dominated* by lust or . . . man *redeemed by Christ*?"[78] In *FC* 34 he stated that married people "cannot . . . look on the law as merely an ideal to be achieved in the future: they must consider it as a command of Christ the Lord to overcome difficulties with constancy." Eduardo Echeverria finds the language of "ideal" and "concrete" in *AL* "inconsistent with the ontological weight of his [Francis'] reference to marriage as being grounded in the normative order of creation" and supportive (even if unwillingly) of the "gradualness of law" theory and of "situation ethics."[79] Although Francis makes a distinction between "the law of gradualness" and "the gradualness of law" (*AL* 295 and 300), Kuljovsky argues that this distinction is simply a "rhetorical device" which is "devoid of meaning"[80] since upon closer analysis of their use in *AL* the two expressions mean one and the same thing.[81] He also considers Francis' use of John Paul II's teaching about "gradualness of law" from *FC* 34 "misleading," since Francis gives the impression that his position elucidated in *AL* can developed from *FC*, while it is in fact in contradiction to the one upheld by John Paul II.[82]

This linguistic shift which juxtaposes the ideal and the real is not the only instance when one cannot help the impression that elements of John Paul II's teaching presented in *VS* are being revisited. In fact, *VS* is not referred to in *AL* at all.[83] While it needs to be admitted that the nature and purpose of these two documents are different (*VS* is in many parts a highly technical document addressed to the bishops of the Catholic Church about certain tendencies in contemporary Catholic moral theology, while *AL* is a pastoral document addressed also to Christian married couples and all the lay faithful), nevertheless, certain linguistic moves seem to be so remarkable that their significance should not be overlooked. Take, for example, John Paul II's statement on intrinsically evil acts and the absolute moral norms which are contained in natural law and, to some extent, are expressed in the Ten Commandments:

> The negative precepts of the natural law are universally valid. They oblige each and every individual, always and in every circumstance. It is a matter of prohibitions which forbid a given action *semper et pro semper*, without exception, because the choice of this kind of behaviour is in no case compatible with the goodness of the will of the acting person, with his vocation to life with God and to communion with his neighbour. It is prohibited – to everyone and in every case – to violate these precepts. They oblige everyone, regardless of the cost, never to offend in anyone, beginning with oneself, the personal dignity common to all.[84]

Or again,

> The negative moral precepts, those prohibiting certain concrete actions or kinds of behaviour as intrinsically evil, do not allow for any legitimate exception. They do not leave room, in any morally acceptable way, for the "creativity" of any contrary determination whatsoever. Once the moral species of an action prohibited by a universal rule is concretely recognized, the only morally good act is that of obeying the moral law and of refraining from the action which it forbids.[85]

Strikingly, when Francis speaks about universal moral norms and their inviolability, his language sounds different:

It is reductive simply to consider whether or not an individual's actions correspond to a general law or rule, because that is not enough to discern and ensure full fidelity to God in the concrete life of a human being . . . It is true that general rules set forth a good which can never be disregarded or neglected, but in their formulation they cannot provide absolutely for all particular situations . . . a pastor cannot feel that it is enough simply to apply moral laws to those living in "irregular" situations . . . "natural law could not be presented as an already established set of rules that impose themselves a priori on the moral subject; rather, it is a source of objective inspiration for the deeply personal process of making decisions."[86]

Or again,

A subject may know full well the rule, yet have great difficulty in understanding "its inherent values" or be in a concrete situation which does not allow him or her to act differently and decide otherwise without further sin. As the Synod Fathers put it, "factors may exist which limit the ability to make a decision."[87]

In other places of *AL* Francis warns against seeing everything in "black and white" (305) and complains that some priests "demand of penitents a purpose of amendment so lacking in nuance that it causes mercy to be obscured by the pursuit of a supposedly pure justice."[88] While he understands "those who prefer a more rigorous pastoral care which leaves no room for confusion" (*AL* 308), he does not agree with them. In fact, he criticises the position of applying general, universal rules to all particular situations (a practice which seems to be quite in line with John Paul II's teachings, as presented earlier) as "hiding behind the Church's teachings, 'sitting on the chair of Moses and judging at times with superiority and superficiality difficult cases and wounded families.'"[89] Such an attitude might lead to using those moral norms as "if they were stones to throw at people's lives."[90]

This brief overview of linguistic shifts and emphases in *AL* suggests that Cardinal Schönborn is correct and something really did change in the Church's rhetoric.[91] From rules which "are universally valid," which "oblige each and every individual, always and in every circumstance," which are "without exception," oblige "everyone and in every case . . . regardless of the cost," which "do not allow for any legitimate exception" and "do not leave room . . . for "creativity of any contrary determination whatsoever" (*VS*), we have arrived at understanding that rules "cannot provide absolutely for all particular situations" and that it is not enough simply to "apply moral laws to those living in 'irregular' situations." From the emphasis that the human person "can never be hindered from not doing certain actions, especially if he is prepared to die rather than to do evil,"[92] we have arrived at understanding that a person might "be in a concrete situation which does not allow him or her to act differently and decide otherwise without further sin" (*AL* 301). While certain qualifications and nuanced distinctions should certainly be made, an overall look at *AL* confirms that it indeed was a "linguistic event."[93] Francis' insistence that "it can *no longer* simply be said that all those in any 'irregular' situation are living in a state of mortal sin and are deprived of sanctifying grace" (*AL* 301, emphasis added) seems to support it – "no longer" means putting a stop to a current mode of speaking and the adoption of a different one. Naturally, it needs to be remembered here that the pre-Francis magisterium did not really say that divorced and civilly remarried couples could not be admitted to the sacraments because they were living in a state of mortal sin and were deprived of sanctifying grace. They could not be admitted to the sacraments because "their state and condition of life objectively contradict that union of love between Christ and the Church which is signified and effected by the Eucharist" and because it would cause scandal (*FC* 84).[94] However, Francis' call for a change of attitude and adopting a new way of thinking and speaking about these people is notable.

Vatican II and *AL* were called "linguistic events," and similarities between them can be seen even in the opening paragraph of the concluding document of Vatican II, Pastoral Constitution on the Church in the Modern World *Gaudium et Spes*, and the opening paragraph of *AL*. The Council states that "[t]he joys and the hopes, the griefs and the anxieties of the men of this age, especially those who are poor or in any way afflicted, these are the joys and hopes, the griefs and anxieties of the followers of Christ,"[95] and Francis opens *AL* with the statement that "[t]he joy of love experienced by families is also the joy of the Church."[96] What John O'Malley recognised as the "panegyric-epideictic genre" of the texts of Vatican II, Thomas Knieps-Port le Roi and Roger Burggraeve recognise also in *AL*. They argue that Francis abandoned the countercultural style of previous magisterial teachings, especially that of John Paul II, and introduced a new way of speaking: "mentality of self-defence and lamentation" and "notoriously pessimistic undertone" are left behind and "[t]he manifest change in tone points to a more substantial reformulation of the message."[97]

O'Malley points out that every successful linguistic event has to have the ability to be contained in a "slogan," that is, a catch phrase which helps to encapsulate the essence of the reform, to be understood by all and to have influence on popular imagination. He explains that such a slogan can serve as a "cheer, [a] loyalty test, [or a] battle cry"[98] and that the adoption of such slogans has precedents in history. During the Gregorian Reform, for example, the slogan adopted by the reformers was "the liberty of the Church" against any undue lay influences. While initially not many contemporaries in the tenth or eleventh centuries would conceive lay influence on the Church as something negative and something from which the Church had to free herself, certain "redefinitions" of such notions as "legitimate authority" and support of "venerable ancient traditions" paved the way to a successful reform. The repeated slogan against which no one could really protest (who would seriously argue against the "liberty of the Church"?) accompanied by the exposing of certain contemporary abuses helped the reform to take root in the popular imagination of Catholics. During the Protestant Reformation, the slogan which became the essence of what the reformers (or at least Luther) were fighting for was "justification by faith alone" or just "the gospel." Again, Luther's program of reform would not have been successful without some "redefinitions" and undue polarisations, but in the end it worked rather well – who could seriously argue against "the gospel" and its priority in Christian teaching and practice?[99]

For Vatican II, such a successful slogan was undoubtedly *aggiornamento*, Pope John XXIII's famous expression encapsulating the reasons for calling the Council and, at the same time, according to many, the Council's most important legacy.[100] On hearing the news about convoking a Council, not all bishops would initially believe that any *aggiornamento* was really necessary for the Church, but after the first sessions of the Council it became an uncontested motto – again, who could seriously argue against the need for the Church to update her methods of teaching and preaching in order to evangelise the rapidly changing world, which needed the liberating message of the Gospel more than ever before?

Can any "slogan" such as these be attached to this particular linguistic event of *AL*? "Discernment" and "inclusion" might be the best possibilities; "mercy" (it occurs at least thirty-five times in the document) and "forgiveness" (twenty-five times) might be also seen as key catchphrases of not only this document, but of Francis's pontificate in general.[101] Just as in the case of the events mentioned earlier, a successful use of these slogans requires some "redefinitions" and repeated emphases. For example, the meaning of the word "discernment" seems to be somehow shifting in the aftermath of *AL*: while for St Ignatius of Loyola, the most well-known proponent of "pastoral discernment" and the founder of the Society of Jesus, the Pope's religious order, it meant choosing only between actions which objectively are either morally good or at least indifferent (that is, not "intrinsically evil"),[102] for Francis it seems to have a broader meaning and apparently can also include, in exceptional cases, a choice of an act which is objectively sinful when no other choice is available.[103]

Also, it was not immediately obvious to everyone that before Francis the Church was not merciful enough and that so many pastors were treating their faithful too harshly. In fact, many would argue the opposite, that is, that on the parish level in many places more common than rigidity were moral and sacramental laxity and general contempt for the Church's official discipline. However, since mistakes in pastoral practices have certainly been made (they always are) and there is always room for improvement, who could argue against the idea of an ever more merciful and compassionate Church which would accompany and help those who find themselves in complex and difficult situations, especially as the number of people finding themselves in those situations is constantly growing?

Notes

1 See Ratzinger, *Theological Highlights of Vatican II*, 106–107, 192.
2 Ibid., 230.
3 A good catalogue of these traditional teachings can be found in Catherine Harmon, "Make Sure You Read These Passages from Amoris Laetitia, Too," *The Catholic World Report* (8 April 2016), www.catholicworldreport.com/Blog/4701/ make_sure_you_read_these_passages_from_iamoris_laetitiai_too.aspx.
4 Available at the official Vatican web page, w2.vatican.va/content/john-paul-ii/ en/apost_exhortations/documents/hf_jp-ii_exh_19811122_familiaris-consortio. html.
5 For an overview of pre-Francis magisterium's position on the matter and the reasons given for upholding this position see Gerhard R. Müller, "Testimony to the Power of Grace: On the Indissolubility of Marriage and the Debate concerning the Civilly Remarried and the Sacraments," in *Remaining in the Truth of Christ: Marriage and Communion in the Catholic Church*, ed. Robert Dodaro, O.S.A. (San Francisco: Ignatius Press, 2014), 148–165; also John Corbett, O.P. et al., "Recent Proposals for the Pastoral Care of the Divorced and Remarried: A Theological Assessment," *Nova et Vetera*, English Edition 12/3 (2014): 601–630.
6 Adam G. Cooper, "The Shape of Repentance: Reflections on *Amoris Laetitia*," *The Catholic World Report* (11 April 2016), www.catholicworldreport.com/ Item/4712/the_shape_of_repentance_reflections_on_iamoris_laetitiai.aspx.
7 Carl E. Olson, "Francis' Sprawling Exhortation a Marriage of Profound and Muddles," *The Catholic World Report* (8 April 2016), www.catholicworldreport.com/Item/4698/francis_sprawling_exhortation_a_marriage_of_profound_and_muddled.aspx.
8 William L. Portier, "A Balancing Act: Reading 'Amoris Laetitia'," *Commonweal* (20 May 2016): 16–18, at 16.
9 Nicholas Austin, S.J., "'Discernment Charged with Merciful Love': Pope Francis' Amoris Laetitia, on Love in the Family," *Thinking Faith* (8 April 2016), www.thinkingfaith.org/articles/discernment-charged-merciful-love-pope-francis%E2%80%99-amoris-laetitia-love-family-0. See also Peter Steinfels, "A Balancing Act: Reading 'Amoris Laetitia'," *Commonweal* (20 May 2016): 13–15, at 13, and Join-Lambert, "Accompanying, Discerning and Integrating the Fragility of Couples," 145–146.

10 Knieps-Port le Roi and Burggraeve, "New Wine in New Wineskins," 285.
11 Examples of these positions will be given in the following pages.
12 Leroy Huizenga, "The Joy of Love in the Hands of the Clergy," *The Catholic World Report* (8 April 2016), www.catholicworldreport.com/Item/4702/ithe_ joy_of_lovei_in_the_hands_of_the_clergy.aspx. Ouellet, "Accompanying, Discerning, Integrating Weakness" states that "chapter 8 is liable to diverging interpretations," adding that these interpretation depend on the reader's acceptance of a law of gradualness (*AL*, 293–295).
13 *AL* 298.
14 *AL* 298 n. 329. Martin M. Lintner, "Divorce and Remarriage: A Reading of Amoris Laetitia from a Theological-Ethical Perspective," in *A Point of No Return?*, 128 argues that "*AL* stops to cite *FC* where its argumentation becomes inconsistent."
15 *GS* 51.
16 Gerald O'Collins, S.J., "The Joy of Love (*Amoris Laetitia*): The Papal Exhortation in Its Context," *Theological Studies* 77 (2016): 905–921, at 918.
17 Lintner, "Divorce and Remarriage," 140.
18 Austin, "'Discernment Charged with Merciful Love'."
19 Basilio Petrà, "From *Familiaris Consortio* to *Amoris Laetitia*: Continuity of the Pastoral Attitude and a Step Forward," in *INTAMS Review* 22 (2016): 202–216, at 211. Doi:10.2143/INT.22.2.3194501.
20 Stephan Kampowski, "In *Amoris Laetitia*, the Family Is an Opportunity, Not a Problem," *The Catholic World Report* (12 April 2016), www.catholicworld report.com/Item/4717/In_iAmoris_Laetitiai_the_family_is_an_opportunity_ not_a_problem.aspx. Kampowski develops his arguments in *Amoris laetitia. Accompagnare discernere integrare* (Siena: Cantagalli, 2016) (co-authored with José Granados and Juan José Pérez-Soba), English edition published as *Accompanying, Discerning, Integrating: A Handbook for the Pastoral Care of the Family According to Amoris Laetitia*, trans. Michael J. Miller (Steubenville, OH: Emmaus Road Publishing, 2017).
21 Olson, "Francis' Sprawling Exhortation".
22 Edward N. Peters, "First Thoughts on the English Version of Pope Francis' *Amoris Laetitia*," *The Catholic World Reporter* (8 April 2016), www.catholic worldreport.com/Blog/4699/dr_edward_peters_first_thoughts_on_the_english_ version_of_pope_francis_amoris_laetitia.aspx.
23 *AL* 305.
24 Tracey Rowland, *Catholic Theology* (London/New York: Bloomsbury T & T Clark, 2017), 198–199.
25 James F. Keenan, S.J., "Receiving *Amoris Laetitia*," *Theological Studies* 78/1 (2017): 193–212, at 199.
26 Francis, *Evangelii Gaudium* (24 November 2013), w2.vatican.va/content/ francesco/en/apost_exhortations/documents/papa-francesco_esortazione- ap_20131124_evangelii-gaudium.html.
27 Edward N. Peters, "The law before 'Amoris' is the law after," *The Catholic World Report* (10 April 2016), www.catholicworldreport.com/Blog/4708/ the_law_before_amoris_is_the_law_after.aspx. Kampowski, "In *Amoris Laetitia*, the Family Is an Opportunity, Not a Problem," is of the same opinion and so is Granados and Pérez-Soba in their *Accompanying, Discerning, Integrating*, 76–78.
28 Code of Canon Law, Can 915, www.vatican.va/archive/ENG1104/_P39.HTM.

29 Peters, "The law before 'Amoris' is the law after."
30 Livio Melina, "First Reflections on *Amoris Laetitia*," www.istitutogp2.it/pub lic/Amoris%20Laetitia-Prime%20riflessioni%20%282016.04.12%29%20 ING.pdf.
31 Austin, "'Discernment Charged with Merciful Love,'" emphasis original.
32 For example, nearly all contributors to *A Point of No Return?* seem to consider it as something obvious. See also Keenan, "Receiving *Amoris Laetitia*," 199; Rocco Buttiglione, "The Joy of Love and the Consternation of Theologians," *L'Osservatore Romano* 29 (22 July 2016): 5.8 and also his *Riposte (amichevoli) ai critici di Amoris Laetitia* (Milan: Ares, 2017) (English translation not available yet).
33 See his remarks at the press conference on his return from Lesvos on 16 April 2016, www.catholicnewsagency.com/news/full-text-of-pope-francis-in-flight-interview-from-lesbos-to-rome-97242/. There might be a number of reasons for Francis' choice of Schönborn for this task; however, the one that is perhaps most worth mentioning is that *AL* "'fully adopted' the pastoral practice regarding remarried divorcees, which has been in use for well over fifteen years in the Vienna archdiocese," which is Schönborn's own diocese (see Keenan, "Receiving *Amoris Laetitia*," 200, referring to Christa Pongratz-Lippitt, "German Group at Family Synod Finds Their Suggestions in Pope's Exhortation," *National Catholic Reporter* (15 April 2016), www.ncronline.org/news/vatican/ german-group-family-synod-finds-their-suggestions-popes-exhortation).
34 Christian Schönborn and Antonio Spadaro, "The Demands of Love," *America* (15–22 August 2016), www.americamagazine.org/issue/demands-love.
35 John Paul II, Encyclical Letter *Veritatis Splendor* (*VS*) (6 August 1993), w2.vatican.va/content/john-paul-ii/en/encyclicals/documents/hf_jp-ii_ enc_06081993_veritatis-splendor.html.
36 The text of the "dubia" can be found at Edward Pentin, "Full Text and Explanatory Notes of Cardinals' Questions on 'Amoris Laetitia'," *National Catholic Register* (14 November 2016), www.ncregister.com/blog/edward-pentin/ full-text-and-explanatory-notes-of-cardinals-questions-on-amoris-laetitia.
37 Louis J. Cameli, "Pope Francis Still Hasn't Responded to the Dubia: He Has Good Reason Not To," *America* (5 January 2017), www.americamagazine. org/faith/2017/01/05/pope-francis-still-hasnt-responded-dubia-he-has-good-reason-not.
38 Gerhard R. Müller, "What Can We Expect from the Family?" Address at conciliar seminary of Oviedo (4 May 2016), http://chiesa.espresso.repubblica.it/ articolo/1351294bdc4.html?eng=y: "If 'Amoris Laetitia' had wanted to eliminate such a deeply rooted and significant discipline, it would have said so clearly and presented supporting reasons." However, according to Müller, no such affirmation can be found in the document and therefore footnote 351 "does not touch the previous discipline: the norm of *FC* 84 and *SC* [*Sacramentum Caritatis* by Benedict XVI, 2006] 29 is still valid, and its application in every case."
39 English translation: Francesco Coccopalmerio, *A Commentary on Chapter Eight of Amoris Laetitia*, trans. Sean O'Neill (New York/Mahwah, NJ: Paulist Press, 2017), 23.
40 Transcript taken from the Vatican web page: *"Francis Rocca of The Wall Street Journal mentioned the recent Post-Synodal Apostolic Exhortation and asked whether or not has been any change in the discipline concerning reception of the sacraments by the divorced and remarried.*

[Francis' response:] I could say "yes" and leave it at that. But that would be too brief a response. I recommend that all of you read the presentation made by Cardinal Schönborn, a great theologian. He is a member of the Congregation for the Doctrine of the Faith and he knows the Church's teaching very well. Your question will find its answer in that presentation. Thank you, w2.vatican. va/content/francesco/en/speeches/2016/april/documents/papa-francesco_ 20160416_lesvos-volo-ritorno.html.

41 *L'Osservatore Romano*, Italian Edition (12 September 2016).
42 "Pope Endorses Argentine Bishops' Document on Amoris Laetitia," http:// en.radiovaticana.va/news/2016/09/12/pope_endorses_argentine_bishops_ document_on_amoris_laetitia/1257635.
43 w2.vatican.va/content/francesco/es/letters/2016/documents/papa-fran cesco_20160905_regione-pastorale-buenos-aires.html.
44 Francis, "Additum Ad Epistulam Region Región Pastoral Buenos Aires", *Acta Apostolicae Saedis* 108 (2016): 1071–1074.
45 Can. 8, §1.
46 Pietro Parolin, "Rescriptum 'Ex Audientia SS.MI," *AAS* 108 (2016): 1074.
47 E.g. Edward Peters, "Pope Francis' Letter to the Argentine Bishops Is in the Acta Apostolicae Sedis: Now What?," *The Catholic World Report* (4 December 2017), www.catholicworldreport.com/2017/12/04/pope-francis-letter-to-the-argentine-bishops-is-in-the-acta-apostolicae-sedis-now-what/; John Joy and Michael Sirilla, "On 'Authentic Magisterium' and the Acta Apostolicae Sedis," *OnePeterFive* (11 December 2017), https://onepeterfive.com/ ep-44-dr-john-joy-dr-michael-sirilla-authentic-magisterium-acta-apostolicae-sedis/; Brian W. Harrison, O.S., "Authentic Confusion over Pope Francis' 'Authentic Magisterium'," *Life Site* (19 December 2017), www.lifesitenews. com/opinion/authentic-confusion-over-pope-francis-authentic-magisterium; Jeffrey Mirus, "The Acta Apostolicae Sedis Is Not an Exercise of the Magisterium of the Church," (19 December 2017), www.catholicculture.org/commen tary/otc.cfm?id=1523; Raymond J. de Souza, "Pope's Amoris Laetitia Guidelines Get an Upgrade," *National Catholic Register* (12 December 2017), www. ncregister.com/daily-news/popes-amoris-laetitia-guidelines-get-an-upgrade.
48 Richard R. Gaillardetz, "Doctrinal Authority in the Francis Era," *Commonweal* (19 December 2016), www.commonwealmagazine.org/doctrinal-authority-francis-era. See also his "In the Service of the People," *The Tablet* (16 April 2016): 6–8 and a longer treatment of the topic in "The Pastoral Orientation of Doctrine," in *Go into the Streets! The Welcoming Church of Pope Francis*, eds. Richard R. Gaillardetz and Thomas Rausch (New York: Paulist Press, 2016), 125–140.
49 Join-Lambert, "Accompanying, Discerning and Integrating the Fragility of Couples," 156.
50 Portier, "A Balancing Act," 16.
51 Lamb, "Francis on the Front Foot," 4.
52 *AL* 305.
53 "Cardinal Schönborn's Intervention at Presentation of *Amoris Laetitia*," http://press.vatican.va/content/salastampa/it/bollettino/pubblico/2016/04/08/ 0241/00531.html#ens.
54 Ibid.
55 Ibid. He refers to *EG* 36.
56 Schönborn, "Presentation of *Amoris Laetitia*."

57 Knieps-Port le Roi and Burggraeve, "New Wine in New Wineskins," 825.
58 Ibid., 286.
59 James Martin, S.J., "Understanding Discernment Is Key to Understanding 'Amoris Laetitia'," *America* (7 April 2016), www.americamagazine.org/issue/discern ment-key-amoris-laetitia, considers discernment to be the "key to understanding 'Amoris Laetitia,' as well as the pope's overall approach to pastoral care." Austin, "'Discernment Charged with Merciful Love'" concurs that "discernment is a hermeneutical key for reading his [Francis'] pontificate to date."
60 Francisco, "Carta del Santo Padre Francisco a los Obispos de la Región Pastoral de Buenos Aires en Respuesta Al Documento 'Criterios Básicos para la Aplicación del Capítulo VIII de la Amoris Laetitia'," w2.vatican.va/content/francesco/es/letters/2016/documents/papa-francesco_20160905_regione-pastorale-buenos-aires.html.
61 Austin, "'Discernment Charged with Merciful Love'."
62 Reinhard Cardinal Marx, "Reflections on the Synod Process and *Amoris Laetitia*," in *A Point of No Return?*, 12–13.
63 *AL* 37.
64 *AL* 303. This particular passage turned out to be one of the most debated passages of the whole document. Josef Seifert, "Does Pure Logic Threaten to Destroy the Entire Moral Doctrine of the Catholic Church?," *Aemaet* 6/2 (2017): 2–9, http://aemaet.de urn:nbn:de:0288-20130928692, 4–6 argues that it "appears to affirm clearly that . . . intrin-sically disordered and objectively gravely sinful acts . . . can be permitted, or can even objectively be commanded, by God" and that "*AL* says that we can know with 'a certain moral security' that God himself asks us to continue to commit intrinsically wrong acts, such as adultery or active homosexuality," which, in his judgment, is a "moral theological atomic bomb that threatens to tear down the whole moral edifice of the 10 commandments and of Catholic Moral Teaching" (at 5). His extended treatment of *AL* can be found in his "Amoris Laetitia: Joy, Sadness and Hopes," *Aemaet* 5/2 (2016): 160–249, http://aemaet.de urn:nbn:de:0288-2015080654. In response to Seifert's publication Archbishop of Granada, Francisco Javier Martínez Fernández, announced that Seifert will be retiring from his Dietrich von Hildebrand Chair for Realist Phenomenology in the International Academy of Philosophy-Instituto de Filosofía Edith Stein. Seifert's response to this action can be found in his "The Persecution of Orthodoxy," *First Things* (5 October 2017), www.firstthings.com/web-exclusives/2017/10/the-persecution-of-ortho doxy. See also Claudio Pierantoni, "Josef Seifert, Pure Logic, and the Beginning of the Official Persecution of Orthodoxy within the Church," *Aemaet* 6/2 (2017): 22–33, http://aemaet.de urn:nbn:de:0288-20130928711; Robert Fastiggi and Dawn Eden Goldstein, "Does Amoris Laetitia 303 Really Undermine Catholic Moral Teaching?," *La Stampa* (26 September 2017), www.lastampa.it/2017/09/26/vaticaninsider/eng/documents/doesamoris-laetitia-really-under mine-catholic-moral-teaching-yom5rmEIfGPzsMDlS7o6eP/pagina.html suggest that *AL* 303 is poorly translated from Latin into English and that the Latin text, unlike the English, is not susceptible of heterodox interpretation. This view was criticised by Christian Brugger (Pete Baklinski, "Yes, Amoris Laetitia 303 Really Undermines Catholic Moral Teaching: Scholar," *Life Site* (6 October 2017), www.lifesitenews.com/news/yes-amoris-laetitia-303-really-undermines-catholic-moral-teaching-scholar. See also Fastiggi/Eden-Goldstein's response and Brugger's response to them at Pete Baklinski, "Theologians Continue Battle over Meaning of Amoris Laetitia 303,"

Life Site (6 October 2017), www.lifesitenews.com/news/theologians-continue-battle-over-meaning-of-amoris-laetitia-303. See also Eduardo Echeverria, "Once Again, 'Amoris Laetitia' §303," *The Catholic World Report* (30 September 2017), www.catholicworldreport.com/2017/09/30/once-again-amoris-laetitia-%C2%A7303/.

65 *AL* 37. For some analysis and various opinions on the treatment of the issue of conscience in *AL* see Michael Lawler and Todd Salzman, "In Amoris Laetitia, Francis' Model of Conscience Empowers Catholics," *National Catholic Reporter* (7 September 2016), www.ncronline.org/news/theology/amoris-laetitia-francis-model-conscience-empowers-catholics and the critique of E. Christian Brugger, who considers the view of conscience presented in *AL* to be more than just a matter of stronger emphasis, but as a revision of the Catholic idea of conscience, see his "The Catholic Conscience, the Argentine Bishops, and 'Amoris Laetitia'." Salzman and Lawler talk about the treatment of conscience in *AL* also in "Amoris Laetitia and Catholic Morals," *The Furrow* 67/12 (December 2016): 666–675, esp. at 666–670 and in *"Amoris Laetitia* and the Development of Catholic Theological Ethics: A Reflection," in *A Point of No Return?*, 30–38. See also Conor M. Kelly, "The Role of the Moral Theologian in the Church: A Proposal in the Light of *Amoris Laetitia*," *Theological Studies* 77/4 (2016): 922–948, esp. 924–929; James T. Bretzke, "There are few, if any, simple 'recipes' for what following a formed and informed conscience looks like," *America* (8 April 2016), www.americamag azine.org/issue/article/good-conscience; Antonio Autiero, *"Amoris laetitia* und das sittliche Gewissen: Eine Frage der Perspektive," in *Amoris laetitia: Wendepunkt in der Moraltheologie?*, eds. Stephan Goertz, and Caroline Witting (Freiburg: Herder, 2016), 95–114; George S. Worgul, *"Amoris Laetitia*: On the Need for a Contextual Theology and Inculturation in Practice," in *A Point of No Return?*, 21–25; Timothy Radcliffe, O.P., "How Can We 'Make Room for the Consciences of the Faithful'?," in *A Point of No Return?*, op. cit., 65–73.

66 At the other side of the spectrum, Nadia Delicata, "Sin, Repentance and Conversion in *Amoris Laetitia*," in *A Point of No Return*, 74–86 finds in *AL* a "robust theology of sin" (at 80 and 86).

67 John Finnis and Germain Grisez, *The Misuse of Amoris Laetitia to Support Errors against the Catholic Faith: A Letter to the Supreme Pontiff Francis, to All Bishops in Communion with Him, and to the Rest of the Christian Faithful* (Indiana: Notre Dame), 17, n. 19; 19, www.twotlj.org/OW-MisuseAL.pdf. Cf. *Catechism of the Catholic Church*, 2384, which states that those who are contracting a new union, even if it is recognised by civil law, are "in a situation of public and permanent adultery."

68 Francis uses the word "irregular" or "irregularity" in the text six times (excluding headings) and uses inverted commas in four of these instances. He does not use them only when he quotes a source which also does not use them.

69 Schönborn, "Presentation of *Amoris Laetitia*."

70 Rowland, *Catholic Theology*, 198.

71 Branislav Kuljovsky, "The Law of Gradualness of the Gradualness of Law? A Critical Analysis of *Amoris Laetitia*," in *A Point of No Return?*, 62, n. 45.

72 Salzman and Lawler, *"Amoris Laetitia* and the Development of Catholic Theological Ethics," 37–38.

73 See *AL* 2, 35, 49, 201, 300, 301, 302, 304, 305 with corresponding footnotes.

74 O'Malley, "Vatican II: Did Anything Happen?," 23.

75 Margaret Hickey, *"Amoris Laetitia*: A Reflection," *The Furrow* 67/9 (September 2016): 482–485, at 482.
76 E. Christian Brugger, "Five Serious Problems with Chapter 8 of *Amoris Laetitia*," *The Catholic World Report* (22 April 2016), www.catholicworldreport.com/Item/4740/five_serious_problems_with_chapter_8_of_iamoris_laetitiai.aspx, section 4.
77 Ibid.
78 *VS* 103 (emphasis original).
79 See his "Chapter 8 of *Amoris Laetitia* and St. John Paul II," *The Catholic World Reporter* (9 April 2016), www.catholicworldreport.com/Item/4706/chapter_8_of_iamoris_laetitiai_and_st_john_paul_ii.aspx.
80 Kuljovsky, "The Law of Gradualness of the Gradualness of Law?," 63–64.
81 Ibid., 46.
82 Ibid., 59.
83 Raymond J. de Souza, "Debating 'Amoris Laetitia': A Look Ahead," *National Catholic Register* (30 December 2016), www.ncregister.com/daily-news/debating-amoris-laetitia-a-look-ahead argues that *VS* is "the principal magisterial document on the moral life since the Council of Trent" and thus "[i]gnoring *Veritatis Splendor* is like writing about the nature of the Church and not making reference to the teaching of Vatican II's dogmatic constitution on the Church, *Lumen Gentium.*"
84 *VS* 52.
85 *VS* 67.
86 *AL* 304–305. Francis is quoting International Theological Commission's, document *In Search of a Universal Ethic: A New Look at Natural Law* (2009), www.vatican.va/roman_curia/congregations/cfaith/cti_documents/rc_con_cfaith_doc_20090520_legge-naturale_en.html, 59.
87 *AL* 301.
88 *AL* 311, n. 364.
89 *AL* 305.
90 Ibid.
91 This is recognised also by Raphael Gallagher, "The Reception of *Amoris Laetitia*," *The Pastoral Review* 12/4 (July/August 2016): 4–9, who mentions a "different tenor" of the document, when compared to previous documents (at 6 and 8).
92 *VS* 52.
93 This change of tone was also noted by such authors as Christopher Lamb, "Compassion Is This Pastor's Watchword," *The Tablet* (16 April 2016): 4–5; Karen Kilby, "Unfinished Business," *The Tablet* (16 April 2016): 8; Megan McCabe, "Pope Francis: We must 'See in the Women's Movement the Working of the Spirit'," *America* (8 April 2016), www.americamagazine.org/issue/article/francis-family-and-feminism.
94 Granados, Kampowski, and Pérez-Soba, *Accompanying, Discerning, Integrating*, 87–88 state that "*it has never been possible to say* what Francis states *can no longer be said*" (emphasis original).
95 *GS* 1.
96 *AL* 1.
97 Knieps-Port le Roi and Burggraeve, "New Wine in New Wineskins," 286–288.
98 O'Malley, "Developments, Reforms and Two Great Reformations," 385.

99 For more on this topic see O'Malley, "Developments, Reforms, and Two Great Reformations," 385–388 and 395–398.
100 O'Malley, "Developments, Reforms, and Two Great Reformations," 396.
101 Portier, "A Balancing Act," 17 states that "[i]f this document has a signature phrase, it is the Ignatian-sounding 'pastoral discernment." Join-Lambert, "Accompanying, Discerning and Integrating the Fragility of Couples," 142 concurs that "'discernment' seems to have become the key word of the pontificate of Pope Francis"; Antonio Spadaro Antonio and Louis J. Cameli, "Watching for God," *America* (1–8 August 2016): 24–27, at 24 agree and also point to "discernment, purification, and reform" as "a tripartite foundation" of the whole pontificate. Ouellet, "Accompanying, Discerning, Integrating Weakness" considers the three verbs from the title of his article to be the summary of Francis' pastoral approach. Walter Kasper, *Pope Francis' Revolution of Tenderness and Love: Theological and Pastoral Perspectives* (New York: Paulist Press, 2015), calls "mercy" the key word of this pontificate (see the whole Chapter V of his book). With regard to ecclesiology of Francis, Lamb argues that the words which encapsulate his general vision of the Church are "collegiality," "synodality" and "subsidiarity," see "Francis on the Front Foot," 4.
102 Joseph A. Tetlow, S.J., *Ignatius Loyola: Spiritual Exercises* (New York: Crossroad, 1992), 122, n. 170.
103 *AL* 301: "A subject may . . . be in a concrete situation which does not allow him or her to act differently and decide otherwise without further sin."

Concluding remarks

As said before, it appears that with the passage of time the number of scholars who argue that *AL* either does not change or cannot change the Church's sacramental policies regarding divorced and civilly remarried Catholics (e.g. Müller, Granados, Kampowski, Pérez-Soba, Peters) is decreasing. The discussion seems to shifting from *if* to *what kind* of change we are witnessing in this pontificate. More and more commentators admit that something did indeed happen with the arrival of *AL* and refer to this change as "development of doctrine." Cardinal Schönborn insists that we are not dealing with any rupture in the Church's teaching or practice, but with "organic development," and he uses John Henry Newman as an ally in his argument.[1] Rocco Buttiglione believes that

> St John Paul II and Pope Francis clearly do not say the same thing but neither do they contradict each other on the theology of marriage. Rather, they are exercising the divinely granted Petrine power of loosening and binding in different ways and in different historical circumstances.[2]

Buttiglione argues that in terms of the notions of the objective state of sin and subjective, personal culpability there is no difference between Francis and the preceding tradition. John Paul II did not say that divorced and civilly remarried Catholics could not be admitted to the sacraments because they were automatically deprived of sanctifying grace, but because they were living in a state of manifest public sin and because admitting them to the sacraments would cause scandal. According to Buttiglione, Pope Francis invites the Church to reconsider this stance, and "the difference between *FC* and *AL* lies completely in this."[3] Furthermore, Buttiglione argues that development of doctrine and practice in this regard had already taken place when John Paul II broke with the previous tradition of considering divorced and civilly remarried Catholics to be automatically excommunicated and when he introduced a novel practice of allowing them to be admitted to the sacraments if they resolve to live in complete continence.[4] Cardinal Kasper argues that another step on this organic development of doctrine and practice was taken by Benedict XVI when he supposedly advised that those who are present at Mass and cannot receive Communion sacramentally can receive it spiritually.[5] Kasper asks: If divorced and civilly remarried can receive the Communion spiritually, why can they not receive it sacramentally?[6]

Schönborn, Buttiglione and Kasper are not the only commentators who believe that the change brought by *AL* was simply a development of doctrine. Rodrigo Guerra López argues that *AL* is "an organic development born out of creative fidelity" and that "there is no discontinuity in the teaching of the most recent Pontiffs."[7] In his opinion, those who argue on the contrary do not interpret St Thomas Aquinas accurately and also do not understand John Paul II.[8] Nicholas Austin states that *AL* "does not mark a rupture in Church teaching" and that "Francis' advocacy of discernment is not a dilution of Church teaching by a 'liberal' pope but a development of a principle acknowledged in the tradition, already present in papal teaching and advocated by the bishops at the two synods."[9] Cardinal Marc Ouellet calls for "creative fidelity to genuine tradition" in the process of application of *AL* and suggests that such "creative fidelity" was exercised by Francis in relation to the practices recommended by *FC* 84.[10] Basilio Petrà opines that while *AL* is in continuity with *FC*, it also "takes a step forward" by looking at the greater tradition of Catholic moral theology which, in his judgement, "holds that the objective contradiction in the penitent's life does not always outweigh the consideration of the penitent's good," which includes the good of the sacraments.[11]

However, not all scholars agree with the view that developments brought about by *AL* are legitimate, not to mention organic. Nicholas J. Healy states that Schönborn's explanation of how *AL* can be derived from the previous teaching is "one-sided and misleading" and that it cannot be squared with John Henry Newman's understanding of development of doctrine.[12] Robert A. Gahl, Jr. thinks that while "Buttiglione's attempt to read *AL* in continuity with the previous papal magisterium is commendable," it remains unconvincing since the proposed pastoral solutions "lead to dangerous and irreconcilable deviations from the tradition" and therefore undermine Buttiglione's very premises.[13] Richard A. Spinello argues that Buttiglione overlooks "a radical discontinuity between Pope Francis and John Paul II on the issue of specific absolute moral norms" and "an acute discordance between *AL* and John Paul II's more measured discussion on subjective culpability."[14] Finally, the 45 signatories of the letter sent in June 2016 to the dean of the College of Cardinals regarding "statements [in *AL*] that can be understood in a sense that is contrary to Catholic faith and morals"[15] and the 250 signatories of *Correctio Filialis* from July 2017 who accuse Francis of "acts, words and omissions which serve to propagate . . . heretical propositions"[16] are also far from admitting that *AL* simply and naturally develops previous teachings.

John O'Malley believes that "development" is simply a "soft word for change."[17] While this statement requires certain qualifications, it is true that every change (or reform) in the Church always includes some levels of both continuity and discontinuity, as Pope Benedict XVI explained in his famous Christmas speech to the Roman Curia about the hermeneutics of the Second Vatican Council.[18] John Henry Newman's image of an acorn growing into an oak tree is certainly a useful image for understanding doctrinal development. However, as noted before, Schönborn's use of Newman is not unproblematic, and the language adopted by *AL* does not make it any easier to argue in this way. Schönborn's account seems to suggest that *AL* takes up what was present in *FC* implicitly and expresses it more explicitly. The Austrian cardinal talks in this context about John Paul II's insistence on the need for "careful discernment of situations" and recognising the "difference between those who have sincerely tried to save their first marriage and have been unjustly abandoned, and those who through their own grave fault have destroyed a canonically valid marriage." He mentions "those who have entered into a second union for the sake of the children's upbringing, and who are sometimes subjectively certain in conscience that their previous and irreparably destroyed marriage had never been valid"[19] as examples of teachings which were already present in John Paul II's teaching implicitly and which were developed by Francis in a more explicit manner. Francis indeed does repeat John Paul's call that those people should "not consider themselves as separated from the Church"[20] and that they should take part in the life of the Church through listening to the word of God, attending Mass, persevering in prayer, works of charity and justice, bringing up children in Christian faith and cultivating the spirit and practice of penance.[21] However, he is going further than this by (1) not repeating John Paul's clear, absolute and unconditional request that they should live like brother and sister, and (2) not repeating his two reasons for this request, that is, that the objective state and condition of life of divorced and remarried contradicts the union which the Eucharist signifies, and that the faithful "would be led into error and confusion regarding the Church's teaching about the indissolubility of marriage."[22] In fact, in relation to the first argument of John Paul II, Francis seems to play it down when he states that

> there is no need to lay upon two limited persons the tremendous burden of having to reproduce perfectly the union existing between Christ and his Church, for marriage as a sign entails "a dynamic process . . . one which advances gradually with the progressive integration of the gifts of God."[23]

Regarding the second argument, Francis admittedly does mention that in the process of bringing about the fuller integration of divorced and civilly remarried persons into the life of the Church any occasion of scandal should be avoided.[24] However, he does not link this with the prohibition of sacramental Communion for them. In fact, as previously mentioned, he does not mention the prohibition at all.

With regard to the use of language, the notion of "organic development" seems to suggest that what is now taught perspicuously was already present essentially in the previous teaching. However, this is not the case here. If in *AL* Francis allows that in some cases divorced and civilly remarried Catholics can receive the Eucharist without the condition of continence, not only does he reverse John Paul II's policy, but he does so *implicitly*. Given the unclear and ambiguous language of this section of *AL* we are dealing here not with a move from general to particular, from vague to precise, from undefined to specific, as Newman would have it, but the reverse. Not only the sacramental policy of the Church changes from rejection of a certain practice to its acceptance (not in all cases, but nevertheless), but also the process of its implementation is inverted: from very precise and unambiguous formulation (admission to the Eucharist is not possible unless the couple lives in continence) we move to a vague, imprecise and undefined idea (the couple should live in continence unless this is impossible in their situation). Even those who are enthusiastic about this change are not particularly enthusiastic about the way it was brought about. Arnaud Join-Lambert complains that Francis "does not make his plea [that access to the sacraments should be made possible for those in irregular situations] in a generalized and undifferentiated way" and compares his language to a matryoshka doll (or Russian doll): in *AL* one can find layers and layers of references and statements which point to other statements, and in this structure it is difficult to find the true meaning of what the Pope is trying to say. Identifying the true meaning of the Pope's statement requires a lengthy journey of exploration, and not every reader will be ready to embark on it.[25] He wonders "if this was the right way to do things, since it risks a confusion that is not favourable to the pastoral exercise of mercy."[26] Thomas Knieps-Port le Roi also endorses the change; however, he calls the Pope's language in *AL*, or at least in certain parts of it, "rather convoluted" and "cryptic."[27] Raymond J. de Souza, a critic of the change, states that "from the first pages of *AL* to the last, the exhortation evidently yearns to declare what it never declares"[28] and that the document "does not engage forthrightly the controverted issue at hand, but rather avoids a direct discussion." He complains that the footnotes of the document are ambiguous, misleading and "do not in fact support the text where they appear, citing only portions of passages to pervert their plain meaning" and describes the way Francis indirectly promulgated the change in *AL* and then supported the

Buenos Aires interpretation as "magisterium by stealth."[29] Claudio Pierantoni states that "relativistic currents of thought and 'situation ethics' which the
previous three Popes had tried hard to stop have now surreptitiously entered
the pages of an official papal document"[30] and that *AL* uses orthodoxy as a
"mask" to conceal situation ethics.[31] Thomas Weinandy, O.F.M., Cap., in his
private letter to the Pope from July 2017 which he decided to make public in
November 2017 and which led to his departure from the office of consultant
to the Committee on Doctrine of the U.S. Conference of Catholic Bishops,
states about Francis' language in Chapter VIII of *AL* that it "at times seems
intentionally ambiguous, thus inviting both a traditional interpretation of
Catholic teaching on marriage and divorce as well as one that might imply a
change in that teaching."[32] Gerald McDermott,[33] Dan Hitchens[34] and Robert
P. Imbelli[35] speak in a similar tone.

Thus, Cardinal Schönborn's and Buttliglione's insistence that there is no
"rupture" here[36] but only "organic development" is not uncontested. Critics of their line of argument believe that it over-softens the impact of this
change and fails to recognise the calibre of this innovation and the extensive
consequences which it will have for the whole Church. These critics think
that the repercussions of this change are better grasped and expressed by
Cardinal Walter Kasper with whom this whole movement of modification
of the Church's discipline is associated. Kasper stated that he "could not
say that *AL* changed *any*thing, because it changed *every*thing"[37] through the
introduction of a "paradigm shift" which will have very significant implications for Catholic moral theology, sacramental theology and pastoral practice.[38] Some bishops and scholars already reacted to this "paradigm shift"
and have stated that if general rules have exceptions, these should be applied
not only to divorced and civilly remarried, but also to other Catholics living
in various irregular situations, for example, to cohabiting couples, homosexual couples or couples practicing contraception.[39] Rather than an end to
a particular discussion, *AL*, just like Vatican II, has already begun to serve
as a new beginning.[40]

First reactions to *AL* are quite similar to first reactions to Vatican II after
its conclusion. In the very same documents of the Council some bishops
saw an upcoming revolution in the Roman Catholic Church, while others saw only minor corrections and a general confirmation of previous
practices and policies. On his return from the last session of the Council, John Charles McQuaid, Archbishop of Dublin and Primate of Ireland,
addressed the Irish Catholics: "You may have been worried by much talk
of changes to come. Allow me to reassure you. No change will worry the
tranquillity of your Christian lives."[41] This has been described as one of
the greatest public misjudgements in Irish history: the Catholic Church
in Ireland underwent an unprecedented change in the decades following

the Council, and the process is not over yet. Is the ambiguous, open-ended, Vatican II–like language of *AL*, combined with the new rhetoric of discernment, welcoming, integration and mercy, going to bring about a change in the Church which could be compared to the one which was brought about by Vatican II? This remains to be seen. However, when one reads Fr Raymond de Souza's opinion that "the magisterial impact of *AL* is limited even in the present and is unlikely to endure in the future" and that "*AL*'s long-term impact will be minimal,"[42] one cannot help wondering whether this is not a misjudgement nearly as serious as that of McQuaid. Admittedly, at this stage it is anyone's guess, but there seem to be good reasons to believe that *AL* will have a profound impact on the whole life of the Church. Gerry O'Hanlon thinks that "the meaning of *AL* goes way beyond the positive teaching on family life that it presents" and believes that "what is at stake here is a new way of being Church, a way that can handle change at all levels (including doctrinal) and yet hope to maintain unity."[43] James Keenan argues that "The Joy of Love is not only calling us to reappropriate the ways we once spoke of conscience, marriage, and penance, but also the way we are the church,"[44] and Monique Baujard calls *AL* a milestone on the way to the synodal church which Francis wants and in which "we all have to learn from each other and where each individual accepts to serve others."[45] To date one of the most visible effects of the document is confusion and division amongst bishops, highest-rank prelates and cardinals, prefects of most important Vatican congregations, episcopal conferences, pastors, theologians and faithful. It is obvious that discussions and exchanges in the Church can often have a stimulating, positive effect on the life of the Church in the long term. However, if this *AL*-related confusion is not dealt with prudently, it could bring regrettable results, as did some aspects of the post–Vatican II reforms which were implemented without a necessary preparation at the ground level.

Up until now, a number of official guidelines have been issued by local church authorities regarding the implementation of *AL*. Many of them promote the view that the document does open the door for the admission of divorced and civilly remarried Catholics to Communion without the absolute requirement of a life of continence. Such local authorities include bishops of Malta,[46] Germany,[47] the Pastoral Region of Buenos Aires,[48] Belgium[49] and the diocese of Rome, the Pope's own diocese.[50] Although there are also guidelines which interpret *AL* differently (including the Archdiocese of Philadelphia,[51] Archdiocese of Portland,[52] Diocese of Portsmouth,[53] Personal Ordinariate of the Chair of Peter,[54] Alberta and Northwest Territories[55]), the Buenos Aires and Roman guidelines have been explicitly and recently publicly endorsed by the Pope. This means that the argument that "nothing has changed in the Church's sacramental discipline" or that "there is no 'before' and 'after' *AL*" is becoming more and more difficult to sustain. Also, with the passage of time and with the new practice becoming increasingly common, it will be more and more difficult to overturn this decision, if hypothetically some future pontiff should wish to do so.

One of the issues which requires further reflection is the question of whether access to the sacraments of Penance and Eucharist for divorced and civilly remarried Catholics who are sexually active in their second unions is to be considered permanent or conditional, that is, should it depend on their resolution to rectify their situation as soon as possible. It is one thing to say that there might be cases in which penitents are (rightly or wrongly, but firmly and thoughtfully) convinced that sexual abstinence is not objectively possible for them *today* for various reasons (e.g. lack of cooperation of one of the partners leading to a real threat of infidelity and destruction of yet another family), but it is quite another to say that it is never going to be possible. Given *AL*'s insistence on the necessity to proclaim the ideal and on the importance of trying to live up to it (*AL* 200, 230, 297, etc.), is it possible to argue that access to the Eucharist might be given to those faithful precisely in order to provide them with strength and nourishment for achieving the ideal (living as brother and sister, if declaration of nullity of the first union is not applicable)? The famous footnote 351 of *AL* talks about "the help of the sacraments." A legitimate question could be asked: help to what end? The text of *AL* 305, to which this footnote refers, states that this ultimate end is "living in God's grace" and "loving and growing in the life of grace and charity." If the Eucharist "is not a prize for the perfect, but a powerful medicine and nourishment for the weak," could it be argued that just like medicine heals sickness and restores to health and nourishment provides strength in the time of frailty, the Eucharist could, in those few, carefully discerned cases, be administered to those Catholics precisely for the same reason, that is, for gradual coming closer to the ideal and, ultimately, arriving at it? The grace of the sacraments of Penance and Eucharist would give those faithful not only the fortitude needed to hold on to their good resolutions, but could also provide them with new insights about possible steps and solutions which can and should be taken up in order to move toward the right direction (the ideal). In this case, the resolution of making everything that is possible and feasible to achieve this ideal would still be a necessary pre-condition for being admitted to these sacraments. It would mean that the process of "dynamic discernment" (*AL* 303) would indeed mean remaining "ever open to new stages of growth and to new decisions which can enable the ideal to be more fully realized" (*AL* 303). It would mean that not only the ideal would not be abandoned, but also that admission to these sacraments would still always require (1) the penitent's recognition of the irregularity of their situation, and (2) the resolution to overcome this irregularity as soon as possible.

It seems that Francis' call for "dynamic discernment" could be read in such way, that is, that access to Communion would in these cases be subject to continuing on the path of discernment, which should always lead from the concrete, not-ideal situation towards the ever-fuller participation in the divine life which the Eucharist symbolises and brings about. In this reading, being in a situation in which the person is convinced that it is not possible to "act differently and decide otherwise without further sin" (*AL* 301) would not be sufficient for being admitted to the sacraments. What would also be required is a genuine resolution of amendment and an honest effort to do everything possible and feasible to change the situation as soon as possible.

Emphasising this aspect might change the growing popular perception that with *AL* "the Church is okaying divorce and extra-marital sex." In this proposed reading the Church would not be okaying anything objectively sinful, even if it was subjectively inculpable. On the contrary, the Church would recognise and name sin for what it is, but she would also extend the means to overcome this sinful situation by providing Eucharistic nourishment to the faithful who are trapped in complex situations from which they genuinely can see no way out. In this reading, the Eucharist would indeed be seen not as a price for the perfect but as a nourishment for the weak; however, this nourishment would have a defined meaning: it would be nourishment *for the way to perfection*, as it should be for all Catholics who receive it, regardless of their situation in life and their "good" or "bad" standing." In other words, the change which *AL* would bring about is that requirement of living continence (*FC* 84) would be changed to requirement of at least a *genuine resolution* to live in continence as soon and as much as possible. This would, of course, apply only to those cases in which the faithful are genuinely (even if falsely) convinced in their conscience that it is not possible to do anything more now in this regard. *FC* 84 appears to expect that at the time of reception of the Eucharist the couple living in an irregular union would have already achieved this goal, whereas *AL* appears to allow the possibility of receiving the Eucharist even before arriving at it, "on the way to it." In this reading, the requirement of a firm resolution to do everything that is possible to achieve this end (the ideal) would still stand and would be necessary for a valid confession.

Such reading and emphasis are certainly exemplary of "restorative reading" of *AL* with which many commentators on both sides of the discussion would not agree. Admittedly, it still does stand in tension with certain aspects of traditional Catholic sacramentology and moral theology, and it does not solve the problem of living in a state and condition of life which objectively contradicts that union of love between Christ and the Church which is signified and effected by the Eucharist (*FC* 84). However, if one wishes to read *AL* through the lenses of the greatest possible continuity with the previous magisterial teaching, in light of Pope Francis' recent words and actions (official endorsement of the Buenos Aires guidelines in *AAS*, the Roman guidelines, personal example), this might be the most conservative reading still possible.

It seems quite likely that Francis will allow this diversity of interpretation of his document to continue, which would be consistent with his principle of decentralisation.[56] However, *that alone* is an important change since no diversity on this matter was allowed before *AL*. The Pope might not *require* officially from pastors that Catholics who are divorced and living in new unions in which they are sexually active be admitted to Communion. However, in *AL* pastors will find permission and encouragement to do it. Before *AL* the position which stated that divorced and remarried Catholics can be admitted to the Eucharist without the absolute requirement of continence was irreconcilable with the official magisterial teaching. It seems that it is not irreconcilable anymore. Before *AL*, if a pastor wanted to be fully obedient to the teaching of the magisterium, he could not admit to the Eucharist those faithful who would not meet this requirement. Now, apparently, he (still) does not have to do this *but he can*. This *is* a significant change, and the manner of introducing it is interestingly similar to the manner in which many post–Vatican II changes were introduced.[57]

A parallel with the topic of the liturgy, which was raised in the introduction to this work, seems to be in place here. After 1970, priests theoretically were not *required* to celebrate Mass *versus populum*, to use only vernacular language, to distribute Communion in the hand, to replace Gregorian chant with popular hymns, etc. However, they *could* do these things with official endorsement of Church authorities and her magisterium. The result was the practical disappearance of the traditional practices mentioned earlier and the adoption of new ones. There are serious reasons to believe that the same is going to happen with the reform brought with *AL*. Also, as with Paul VI's liturgical reform, the consequences of Francis' reform will be highly significant, not only on the level of pastoral practice, but also on the level of doctrine and magisterial teaching. In his comment on *AL* Nihal Abeyasingha lists the five stages of development of doctrine identified by Humphrey O'Leary: (1) the subject is not mentioned, (2) the practice is outright rejected, (3) some practice is allowed as an exception, (4) an exception is encouraged, (5) the exception becomes the norm.[58] If this description is correct and can be applied to *AL*, we have just entered the third stage. Cardinals Kasper and Marx, on the one hand, and Müller or Burke, on the other, might differ drastically in their evaluation of *AL*, but they seem to agree on this one point, that is, that something of at least a "minor earthquake" has taken place. They also realise and agree that the stakes are higher than many might conceive today and that this is not only a discussion about a particular issue related to a particular discipline or policy, but ultimately a discussion about the shape of the Church in general.

Pope Francis expressed his hope that Chapter VIII of *AL* would challenge everyone (*AL* 7) and that attempts at its implementation would make our lives "wonderfully complicated" (*AL* 308). While not everyone would agree about the wonderfulness of this complication, few would deny that this particular aim of the document was certainly achieved.

Notes

1 Schönborn, "Presentation of *Amoris Laetitia*" in Gerard O'Connell, "'Amoris Laetitia' Represents an Organic Development of Doctrine, 'Not a Rupture,'" *America* (8 April 2016), www.americamagazine.org/faith/2016/04/08/amoris-laetitia-represents-organic-development-doctrine-not-rupture.
2 Buttiglione, "The Joy of Love and the Consternation of Theologians," 8.
3 Ibid., 8.
4 Ibid., 5.
5 Cf. Benedict XVI, *Sacramentum Caritatis*, 55.
6 See his famous speech at the extraordinary consistory of cardinals on marriage and the family on 20 February 2014, in anticipation of the Synod of Bishops, to be found in Walter Kasper, *The Gospel of the Family*, trans. William Madges (Mahwah, NJ: Paulist Press, 2014), 30. For a critical analysis of this proposal see Juan José Pérez-Soba and Stephan Kampowski, *The Gospel of the Family: Going Beyond Cardinal Kasper's Proposal in the Debate on Marriage, Civil Re-Marriage and Communion in the Church*, trans. Michael J. Miller (San Francisco: Ignatius Press, 2014), esp. 149–154. Paul Jerome Keller, O.P., "Is Spiritual Communion for Everyone?," *Nova et Vetera*, English, Edition 12/3 (2014): 631–655 provides a fine analysis of the notion of spiritual Communion in history, including an important distinction between "Communion of desire" and "desire of Communion." At the same time, he reluctantly admits that *Sacramentum Caritatis can* be read in a way which would allow divorced and civilly remarried to receive "Communion of desire" (he complains about "insufficiently precise drafting" of *Sacramentum Caritatis* and of its "infelicitous" use of the term "spiritual communion," see pp. 641 and 645).
7 Rodrigo Guerra López, "The Relevance of Some Reflections by Karol Wojtyła for Understanding Amoris Laetitia: Creative Fidelity," *L'Osservatore Romano* (22 July 2016), www.osservatoreromano.va/en/news/relevance-some-reflections-karol-wojtyla-understan.
8 Ibid.
9 Austin, "Not All Is Black and White," 8.
10 Ouellet, "Accompanying, Discerning, Integrating Weakness."
11 Petrà, "From *Familiaris Consortio* to *Amoris Laetitia*," 212–213.
12 Nicholas J. Healy, "The Light of Faith and the Development of Doctrine," *Anthropotes* 22 (2017): 197–214, at 212–214.
13 Robert A. Gahl, Jr., "A Response to Rocco Buttiglione's Reading of Amoris Laetitia," *First Things* (26 July 2016), www.firstthings.com/web-exclusives/2016/07/healing-through-repentance.
14 Richard A. Spinello, "On Rocco Buttiglione's Defense of Amoris Laetitia," *Crisis Magazine* (9 August 2016), www.crisismagazine.com/2016/rocco-buttiglione-defense-amoris-laetitia.
15 See "Amoris Laetitia: Critical Analysis," (29 June 2016), http://sspx.org/en/amoris-laetitia-critical-analysis.

16 www.correctiofilialis.org/wp-content/uploads/2017/08/Correctio-filialis_English_
1.pdf., 3.

17 O'Malley, "Vatican II: Did Anything Happen?," 9.

18 Benedict XVI, "Christmas Address to the Roman Curia (22 December 2005),"
L'Osservatore Romano, Weekly Edition in English 1 (4 January 2006): 4–6.

19 *FC* 84.

20 Francis says that they should not feel "excommunicated" three times in *AL* para.
243, 246 and 299. The current Code of Canon Law explains that the excommunicated person cannot "have any ministerial participation in celebrating the sac-
rifice of the Eucharist or any other ceremonies of worship whatsoever" (which
cannot refer to divorced and remarried Catholics anyway), and that they cannot "celebrate the sacraments or sacramentals and to receive the sacraments"
or "exercise any ecclesiastical offices, ministries, or functions whatsoever or to
place acts of governance" (Can. 1331 §1). One can imagine that an argument
could be made that (1) if only excommunicated persons cannot receive sacraments "out of principle" and (2) divorced and remarried are not excommunicated, therefore their exclusion from the sacramental life should not be assumed
"out of principle" but rather should take into account each case individually.
Arnaud Join-Lambert seems to argue this manner in "Accompanying, Discerning and Integrating the Fragility of Couples," 149–151.

21 *FC* 84.

22 *FC* 84. See also the Declaration of Pontifical Council for Legislative
Texts, "II. Concerning the Admission to Holy Communion of Faithfull Who Are
Divorced and Remarried," (24 June 2000), www.vatican.va/roman_curia/
pontifical_councils/intrptxt/documents/rc_pc_intrptxt_doc_20000706_dec
laration_en.html, which develops the idea of "public unworthiness" of those
couples, and the Congregation for the Doctrine of the Faith's, "Letter to the
Bishops of the Catholic Church Concerning the Reception of Holy Communion
by the Divorced and Remarried Members of the Faithful," (14 September 1994),
www.vatican.va/roman_curia/congregations/cfaith/documents/rc_con_cfaith_
doc_14091994_rec-holy-comm-by-divorced_en.html, which reiterates the teaching of John Paul II from *FC* 84 and confirms that "this practice, which is
presented as binding, cannot be modified because of different situations" (sec. 5).

23 *AL* 122. The second part of the sentence is a quotation from *FC* 9. Portier, "A Balancing Act," 18, considers this statement of Francis' to be "the most theologically
important passage in this document." For a more detailed study of the topic of (too
high) expectations from married couples in *AL* see Stephanie Höllinger, "Do We
Expect Too Much? A Reflection on Expectations and Marriage in *Amoris Laetitia*," in *A Point of No Return?*, 103–119. Surprisingly, however, in her analysis
Höllinger does not refer to Francis' treatment of Eph 5:21–33.

24 *AL* 299.

25 Join-Lambert, "Accompanying, Discerning and Integrating the Fragility of Couples," 152–153.

26 Ibid., 154.

27 Corinne Bernhard-Bitaud and Thomas Knieps-Port le Roi, "'Nourishment for
the Journey, Not a Prize for the Perfect': Reflecting with *Amoris Laetitia* on
Eucharistic Sharing in Interchurch Marriages," in *A Point of No Return?*, 227
and 232.

28 Raymond J. de Souza, "'Amoris Laetitia,' the Holy Spirit and the Synod of
Surprises," *National Catholic Register* (8 April 2016), www.ncregister.com/
daily-news/amoris-laetitia-the-holy-spirit-and-the-synod-of-surprises.

29 de Souza, "Debating 'Amoris Laetitia'." Not only critics of *AL* note Francis' way of quoting sources in a way which does not really correspond to what he argues. Knieps-Port le Roi and Burggraeve, "New Wine in New Wineskins" point that with regard to *AL* 120, "Francis explicitly refers to this tradition [regarding the grace of the sacrament of marriage, *FC* 13] but [then] forcefully goes against it" and that on another occasion the quote taken from *FC* 9 is torn out of context in which it was used there (p. 293, also in n. 24). With regard to *AL* 303 and its reference to the Pontifical Council for Legislative Texts, *Declaration Concerning the Admission to Holy Communion of Faithful Who Are Divorced and Remarried* (2000), they state that "[w]e are faced here with another instance where Pope Francis quotes previous church teaching but in fact modifies – or as in this case, inverts – its meaning" (p. 298, n. 33).

30 Pierantoni, "Josef Seifert, Pure Logic, and the Beginning of the Official Persecution of Orthodoxy within the Church," 28.

31 Diane Montagna, "Amoris Laetitia Uses Orthodoxy as 'Mask' to Conceal Moral Errors: Catholic Philosopher," *Life Site* (10 October 2017), www.lifesitenews. com/news/amoris-laetitia-uses-orthodoxy-as-mask-to-conceal-moral-errors-catholic-phi. The authorised Italian text of the interview can be found at https:// s3.amazonaws.com/lifesite/ITALIAN_VERSION-_INTERVIEW_WITH_CLAU DIO_PIERANTONI__RESPONDING_TO_ROCCO_BUTTIGLIONE.pdf.

32 Thomas G. Weinandy, O.F.M., Cap., "Letter to Pope Francis," (31 July 2017), https://cruxnow.com/wp-content/uploads/2017/10/Francis-Letter-Final.pdf. Weinandy, Seifert, Harrison, signatories of *Correctio Filialis* and other critics of *AL* have often been described as "dissenters" (e.g. James Martin, "Dissent, Now & Then: Thomas Weinandy and the Meaning of Jesuit Discernment," *America* (3 November 2017), www.americamagazine.org/faith/2017/11/03/ dissent-now-then-thomas-weinandy-and-meaning-jesuit-discernment). While this expression might be technically correct, certain distinctions need to be made, most importantly regarding the reason for dissent. It is one thing to dissent from the magisterial teaching because it does not change its traditional positions (e.g. the dissent following the publication of *Humanae Vitae* in 1968), and it is quite another to dissent because it does.

33 Gerald McDermott, "Is Pope Francis a Liberal Protestant?," *First Things* (15 November 2017), www.firstthings.com/web-exclusives/2017/11/is-pope-francis-a-liberal-protestant.

34 Dan Hitchens, "A Time of Crisis," *First Things* (30 October 2017), www.firstthings. com/web-exclusives/2017/10/a-time-of-crisis.

35 Robert P. Imbelli, "The Principled Ambivalence of Pope Francis," *First Things* (7 November 2017), www.firstthings.com/web-exclusives/2017/11/ the-principled-ambivalence-of-pope-francis.

36 Schönborn probably uses this expression to reiterate Benedict XVI's rejection of "hermeneutics of rupture" as described in his 22 December 2005 speech. Austin, "'Discernment Charged with Merciful Love'" speaks in a similar tone to him when he states that "Francis does not *change* the content of church teaching on marriage and family; he *transposes* it from the key of law to that of virtue, and makes the primacy of love clearer once again" (emphases original).

37 *The Tablet* (16 April 2016), 25.

38 Walter Kasper, "'Amoris Laetitia': Bruch Oder Aufbruch? Eine Nachlese," *Stimmen der Zeit* 234 (2016): 723–732. In similar fashion, Russell Pollitt, S.J., "Bishops of South Africa Welcome Pope Francis' Exhortation," *America* (8 April 2016), www.americamagazine.org/content/dispatches/popes-exhorta

tion-welcomed-south-africa talks about "redirecting of the Catholic mindset," "a mind shift for all Catholics" and embarking on a new process, that is changing the way all Catholics think about themselves.

39 Diane Montagna, "New Academy for Life Member Uses Amoris to Say Some Circumstances 'Require' Contraception," *Life Site* (8 January 2018), www. lifesitenews.com/news/new-academy-for-life-member-uses-amoris-to-say-some-circumstances-require-c. Whether there really is a radical paradigm shift in the moral theology of Pope Francis is a question which deserves a separate study.

40 Imbelli links this with Francis' own statement from *EG* 223 about the importance of "initiating processes rather than possessing spaces" where spaces are understood here as "power and of self-assertion." See his "The Principled Ambivalence of Pope Francis."

41 *The Irish Times*, 10 December 1965, quoted in Dermot A. Lane, "Vatican II: The Irish Experience," *The Furrow* 55/2 (February 2004): 67–81, at 67.

42 Raymond de Souza, "Amoris Laetitia Is Destined to Be Forgotten," *The Catholic Herald* (30 September 2017), www.catholicherald.co.uk/issues/september-30th-2016/amoris-laetitia-is-destined-to-be-forgotten/.

43 Gerry O'Hanlon, "The Joy of Love: '*Amoris Laetitia*'," *The Furrow* 67/6 (June 2016): 328–336, at 336.

44 Keenan, "Receiving *Amoris Laetitia*," 221.

45 Monique Baujard, "Existing Practices and New Initiatives for the Divorced and Remarried in France," in *A Point of No Return?*, 246. On the other hand, Rita Ferrone, "No Stalemate: What Historians Will Say about Francis," *Commonweal* (8 September 2017): 8 opines that "history will look on Pope Francis's post-synodal exhortation *AL* (2016) as a very modest gesture toward a more humane pastoral approach to marriage," that "flexibility and accompaniment recommended by the Pope is not outside the scope of church teaching" and that "[a]nxiety about rules-making and rules-keeping has magnified the controversy over communion (something which has always been subject to discernment in the 'internal forum') far beyond its actual weight."

46 http://ms.maltadiocese.org/WEBSITE/2017/PRESS%20RELEASES/Norms%20for%20the%20Application%20of%20Chapter%20VIII%20of%20AL.pdf.

47 www.dbk.de/fileadmin/redaktion/diverse_downloads/presse_2017/2017-015a-Wortlaut-Wort-der-Bischoefe-Amoris-laetitia.pdf.

48 See n. 130 earlier.

49 www.cathobel.be/wp-content/uploads/2017/05/2017-05-09-Amoris-laetitia-Lettre-pastorale.pdf.

50 www.romasette.it/wp-content/uploads/Relazione2016ConvegnoDiocesano.pdf.

51 http://archphila.org/wp-content/uploads/2016/06/AOP_AL-guidelines.pdf.

52 http://archdpdx.org/documents/2016/10/PASTORAL%20LETTER%20A%20True%20and%20Living%20Icon%20FINAL-1.pdf.

53 www.portsmouthdiocese.org.uk/bishop/docs/20160424-BoP-Pastoral-Message-Amoris-Laetitia.pdf.

54 https://ordinariate.net/letters-and-statements.

55 https://caedm.ca/Portals/0/documents/family_life/2016-09-14_PastoralAccompanimenttoDivorcedandRemarried.pdf.

56 *AL* 3; *EG* 16. Gemma Simmonds, "Amoris Laetitia: A View from the Female Bridge," *Thinking Faith* (13 May 2016), www.thinkingfaith.org/articles/amoris-laetitia-%E2%80%93-view-female-bridge states that "the whole approach of

Amoris Laetitia suggests that these decisions [made within the 'messy, complex and often contradictory reality in which families live'] cannot be imposed in a totalitarian sense from above but must be personally and pastorally discerned, within their context, by those primarily affected." Archbishop William Slattery stated that the Pope's refusal to propose particular solutions "may seem a radical step to those unfamiliar with the history of a church that we have grown to see as highly centralized, with doctrines, laws and practices sent down from on high to us to be applied in every case," see Kevin Clarke, "An 'Ill-Judged Shift' or a New 'Pastoral Mind-Set'? Different Takes on 'Amoris Laetitia'," *America* (8 April 2016), www.americamagazine.org/issue/reactions-roll-apostolic-exhortation-pope-francis.

57 Ross Douthat, "The Confusion of Conservative Catholics," seems to argue in this manner. Critics of *AL* sometimes argue that "authentic magisterium" is not infallible and, therefore, it does not have to be accepted with the same level of obedience as *ex-cathedra* teachings. While this is true, it needs to be remembered that (1) this level of teaching does require "religious submission of will and intellect" (*LG* 25, *CIC* 752) and that (2) the majority of cases of post–Vatican II, public theological dissent also concerned non-infallible teachings. Emphasising the "right to dissent" from Francis' magisterium begs the question about the "right to dissent" from the magisterium of the previous popes.

58 Nihal Abeyasingha, "Amoris Laetitia and Sensus Fidelium," *Compass* 50/4 (Summer 2016): 29–41, at 30.

Bibliography

Abeyasingha, Nihal. "Amoris Laetitia and Sensus Fidelium." *Compass* 50/4 (Summer 2016): 29–41.

Alberigo, Giuseppe. "VIII: Transition to a New Age." In *History of Vatican II, Vol. 5: The Council and the Transition: The Fourth Period and the End of the Council, September 1965–December 1965*, English Version edited by Joseph A. Komonchak. Translated by Matthew J. O'Connel, 573–644. Maryknoll, NY: Orbis Books/ Leuven: Peeters, 2006.

Amerio, Romano. *Iota Unum: A Study of Change in the Catholic Church in the Twentieth Century*. Translated by John P. Parson. Kansas City, MO: Sarto House, 1996.

"Amoris Laetitia: Critical Analysis." Letter of 45 Theologians, Philosophers, Church Historians and Pastors. (29 June 2016). http://sspx.org/en/amoris-laetitia-critical-analysis.

Ascerbi, Antonio. "Receiving Vatican II in a Changes Historical Context." *Concilium* 146 (1981): 77–84.

Austin, Nicholas. "'Discernment Charged with Merciful Love': Pope Francis' Amoris Laetitia, on Love in the Family." *Thinking Faith* (8 April 2016). www.thinkingfaith. org/articles/discernment-charged-merciful-love-pope-francis%E2%80%99-amoris-laetitia-love-family-0.

Austin, Nicholas. "Not All Is Black and White." *The Tablet* (8 April 2017): 8–9.

Baklinski, Pete. "Theologians Continue Battle over Meaning of Amoris Laetitia 303." *Life Site* (6 October 2017). www.lifesitenews.com/news/theologians-continue-battle-over-meaning-of-amoris-laetitia-303.

Baklinski, Pete. "Yes, Amoris Laetitia 303 Really Undermines Catholic Moral Teaching: Scholar." *Life Site* (6 October 2017). www.lifesitenews.com/news/yes-amoris-laetitia-303-really-undermines-catholic-moral-teaching-scholar.

Baujard, Monique. "Existing Practices and New Initiatives for the Divorced and Remarried in France." In *A Point of No Return?* Amoris Laetitia *on Marriage, Divorce and Remarriage*, 242–246.

Benedict XVI, Pope. "Christmas Address to the Roman Curia, (22 December 2005)." *L'Osservatore Romano, Weekly Edition in English* 1 (4 January 2006): 4–6.

Benedict XVI, Pope. *Post-Synodal Exhortation on the Eucharist, Sacramentum Caritatis.* London: Catholic Truth Society, 2007.

Bernhard-Bitaud, Corinne and Thomas Knieps-Port le Roi. " 'Nourishment for the Journey, Not a Prize for the Perfect': Reflecting with *Amoris Laetitia* on Eucharistic Sharing in Interchurch Marriages." In *A Point of No Return? Amoris Laetitia on Marriage, Divorce and Remarriage,* 215–232.

Biliniewicz, Mariusz. "*Sacrosanctum Concilium*: A Review of the Theological Critique." In *Sacrosanctum Concilium: Sacred Liturgy and the Second Vatican Council: Proceedings of the Sixth Fota International Liturgical Conference, 2013: Essays in Commemoration of the Fiftieth Anniversary of the Promulgation of the Conciliar Constitution. 1963–2013,* edited by John M. Cunningham, O.P., 71–90. Wells, Somerset: Smenos, 2015.

Bretzke, James T. "There Are Few, If Any, Simple 'Recipes' for What Following a Formed and Informed Conscience Looks Like." *America* (8 April 2016). www. americamagazine.org/issue/article/good-conscience.

Brugger, E. Christian. "The Catholic Conscience, the Argentine Bishops, and 'Amoris Laetitia'." *The Catholic World Report* (20 September 2016). www. catholicworldreport.com/Item/5069/the_catholic_conscience_the_argentine_bishops_and_amoris_laetitia.aspx.

Brugger, E. Christian. "Five Serious Problems with Chapter 8 of *Amoris Laetitia*." *The Catholic World Report* (22 April 2016). www.catholicworldreport.com/Item/4740/five_serious_problems_with_chapter_8_of_iamoris_laetitiai.aspx.

Buttiglione, Rocco. "The Joy of Love and the Consternation of Theologians." *L'Osservatore Romano, Weekly English Edition* 29 (22 July 2016): 5–8.

Caffara, Carlo. "Sacramental Ontology and the Indissolubility of Marriage." In *Remaining in the Truth of Christ: Marriage and Communion in the Catholic Church,* 166–180.

Cameli, Louis J. "Pope Francis Still Hasn't Responded to the Dubia: He Has Good Reason Not to." *America* (5 January 2017). www.americamagazine.org/faith/2017/01/05/pope-francis-still-hasnt-responded-dubia-he-has-good-reason-not.

Catechism of the Catholic Church, 2nd ed. Strathfield, NSW: St Pauls, 2000.

Chaput, Charles J. "Pastoral Guidelines for Implementing *Amoris Laetitia*." Archdiocese of Philadelphia, 2016. http://archphila.org/wp-content/uploads/2016/06/AOP_AL-guidelines.pdf.

Clarke, Kevin. "An 'Ill-Judged Shift' or a New 'Pastoral Mind-Set'? Different Takes on 'Amoris Laetitia'." *America* (8 April 2016). www.americamagazine.org/issue/reactions-roll-apostolic-exhortation-pope-francis.

Coccopalmerio, Francesco. *A Commentary on Chapter Eight of Amoris Laetitia.* Translated by Sean O'Neill. New York/Mahwah, NJ: Paulist Press, 2017.

Code of Canon Law. www.vatican.va/archive/ENG1104/_P39.HTM.

Congregation for the Doctrine of the Faith. "Letter to the Bishops of the Catholic Church Concerning the Reception of Holy Communion by the Divorced and Remarried Members of the Faithful." (14 September 1994). www.vatican.va/roman_curia/congregations/cfaith/documents/rc_con_cfaith_doc_14091994_rec-holy-comm-by-divorced_en.html.

Cooper, Adam G. "The Shape of Repentance: Reflections on *Amoris Laetitia*." *The Catholic World Report* (11 April 2016). www.catholicworldreport.com/Item/4712/the_shape_of_repentance_reflections on_iamoris_laetitiai.aspx.

Corbett, John, O.P., Dominic Legge, O.P., Andrew Hofer, O.P., Kurt Martens, Paul J. Keller, O.P., Thomas Petri, O.P., Dominic Langevin, O.P. and Thomas Joseph White, O.P. "Recent Proposals for the Pastoral Care of the Divorced and Remarried: A Theological Assessment." *Nova et Vetera*, English Edition 12/3 (2014): 601–630.

Correctio filialis de haeresibus propagatis. (16 July 2017). www.correctiofilialis.org/wp-content/uploads/2017/08/Correctio-filialis_English_1.pdf.

Correia, Frances. "My Personal Experience of Marriage and Amoris Laetitia." *Jesuit Institute South Africa.* (15 April 2016). www.jesuitinstitute.org.za/index.php/2016/04/15/my-personal-experience-of-marriage-and-amoris-laetitia/.

Davies, Michael. *Liturgical Time Bombs In Vatican II: Destruction of the Faith through Changes in Catholic Worship.* Charlotte, NC: Tan Books, 2003.

Delicata, Nadia. "Sin, Repentance and Conversion in Amoris Laetitia." In *A Point of No Return? Amoris Laetitia on Marriage, Divorce and Remarriage*, 74–86.

De Paolis, Velasio. "The Divorced and Civilly Remarried and the Sacraments of the Eucharist and Penance." In *Remaining in the Truth of Christ: Marriage and Communion in the Catholic Church*, 181–209.

Der Deutschen Bischofskonferenz. "Die Freude der Liebe, die in den Familien gelebt wird, ist auch die Freude der Kirche: Einladung zu einer erneuerten Ehe– und Familienpastoral im Licht von Amoris Laetitia." Pressemitteilungen Der Deutschen Bischofskonferenz, 2017. www.dbk.de/fileadmin/redaktion/diverse_downloads/presse_2017/2017-015a-Wortlaut-Wort-der-Bischoefe-Amoris-laetitia.pdf.

de Souza, Raymond J. "'Amoris Laetitia', the Holy Spirit and the Synod of Surprises." *National Catholic Register* (8 April 2016). www.ncregister.com/daily-news/amoris-laetitia-the-holy-spirit-and-the-synod-of-surprises.

de Souza, Raymond J. "Amoris Laetitia Is Destined to Be Forgotten." *The Catholic Herald* (30 September 2017). www.catholicherald.co.uk/issues/september-30th-2016/amoris-laetitia-is-destined-to-be-forgotten/.

de Souza, Raymond J. "Debating 'Amoris Laetitia': A Look Ahead." *National Catholic Register* (30 December 2016). www.ncregister.com/daily-news/debating-amoris-laetitia-a-look-ahead.

de Souza, Raymond J. "Pope's Amoris Laetitia Guidelines Get an Upgrade." *National Catholic Register* (12 December 2017). www.ncregister.com/daily-news/popes-amoris-laetitia-guidelines-get-an-upgrade.

Di Nicola, Giulia P. and Attilio Danese. "Notes on *Amoris Laetitia*." *INTAMS Review* 22: 3–14. Doi: 10.2143/INT.22.1.3159713.

Dodaro, Robert, O.S.A., ed. *Remaining in the Truth of Christ: Marriage and Communion in the Catholic Church.* San Francisco: Ignatius Press, 2014.

Dossetti, Giuseppe. "Per una valutazione globale del magistero del Vaticano II." In *Il Vaticano II: Frammenti di una riflessione*, edited by F. Margiotta Broglio. Bologna: Il Mulino, 1996.

Douthat, Ross. "The Confusion of Conservative Catholics." *The New York Times* (19 April 2016). https://douthat.blogs.nytimes.com/2016/04/19/the-confusion-of-conservative-catholics/.

Dulles, Avery. "From Ratzinger to Benedict." *First Things* 160 (February 2006): 24–29.

Dulles, Avery. "Vatican II: The Myth and the Reality." *America* (24 February 2003): 7–11.

Dulles, Avery. "Vatican II: Substantive Teaching: A Reply to John W. O'Malley and Others." *America* (31 March 2003): 14–17.

Echeverria, Eduardo. "Chapter 8 of *Amoris Laetitia* and St. John Paul II." *The Catholic World Report* (9 April 2016). www.catholicworldreport.com/Item/4706/chapter_8_of_iamoris_laetitiai_and_st_john_paul_ii.aspx.

Echeverria, Eduardo. "Once Again, 'Amoris Laetitia' §303." *The Catholic World Report* (30 September 2017). www.catholicworldreport.com/2017/09/30/once-again-amoris-laetitia-%C2%A7303/.

Egan, Philip. "*Pastoral Message from Bishop Philip about the Apostolic Exhortation,* 'Amoris Laetitia' (*'The Joy of Love'*)." Portsmouth, 2016. www.portsmouth diocese.org.uk/bishop/docs/20160424-BoP-Pastoral-Message-Amoris-Laetitia. pdf.

Faggioli, Massimo. *A Council for the Global Church: Receiving Vatican II in History.* Augsburg, MN: Fortress Press, 2015.

Faggioli, Massimo. "Quaestio Disputata: *Sacrosanctum Concilium* and the Meaning of Vatican II." *Theological Studies* 71 (2010): 437–452.

Faggioli, Massimo. *Vatican II: The Battle for Meaning.* New York/Mahwah, NJ: Paulist Press, 2012.

Faggioli, Massimo. "Vatican II: History and Narratives." *Theological Studies* 73 (2012): 749–767.

Fastiggi, Robert and Dawn Eden Goldstein. "Critics of Amoris Laetitia Ignore Ratzinger's Rules for Faithful Theological Discourse." *La Stampa* (13 October 2017). www.lastampa.it/2017/10/04/vaticaninsider/eng/documents/critics-of-amoris-laetitia-ignore-ratzingers-rules-for-faithful-theological-discourse-gPj2TR3u19 CUW8PI0vr4L/pagina.html.

Fastiggi, Robert and Dawn Eden Goldstein. "Does Amoris Laetitia 303 Really Undermine Catholic Moral Teaching?" *La Stampa* (26 September 2017). www. lastampa.it/2017/09/26/vaticaninsider/eng/documents/doesamoris-laetitia-really-undermine-catholic-moral-teaching-yom5rmEIfGPzsMDlS7o6eP/pagina.html.

Ferrara, Christopher A. "Wait! Wait! It's All a Mistranslation!" *The Remnant* (1 October 2017). https://remnantnewspaper.com/web/index.php/articles/item/3450-wait-wait-it-s-all-a-mistranslation.

Ferrone, Rita. "No Stalemate: What Historians Will Say about Francis." *Commonweal* (8 September 2017): 8.

Finnis, John and Germain Grisez. "The Misuse of *Amoris Laetitia* to Support Errors against the Catholic Faith: A Letter to the Supreme Pontiff Francis, to All Bishops in Communion with Him, and to the Rest of the Christian Faithful." Indiana: Notre Dame, 2016. www.twotlj.org/OW-MisuseAL.pdf.

68   *Bibliography*

Francis, Pope. "Additum Ad Epistulam Region Región Pastoral Buenos Aires." *Acta Apostolicae Saedis* 108 (2016): 1071–1074.

Francis, Pope. "Apostolic Exhortation *Evangelii Gaudium*." (24 November 2013). w2.vatican.va/content/francesco/en/apost_exhortations/documents/papa-francesco_esortazione-ap_20131124_evangelii-gaudium.html.

Francis, Pope. "Carta del Santo Padre Francisco a los Obispos de la Región Pastoral de Buenos Aires en Respuesta Al Documento 'Criterios Básicos para la Aplicación del Capítulo VIII de la Amoris Laetitia'." w2.vatican.va/content/fran cesco/es/letters/2016/documents/papa-francesco_20160905_regione-pastorale-buenos-aires.html.

Francis, Pope. "Post-Synodal Apostolic Exhortation on Love in the Family *Amoris Laetitia*." (19 March 2016). w2.vatican.va/content/dam/francesco/pdf/apost_exhortations/documents/papa-francesco_esortazione-ap_20160319_amoris-laetitia_en.pdf.

Gahl, Robert A., Jr. "A Response to Rocco Buttiglione's Reading of Amoris Laetitia." *First Things* (26 July 2016). www.firstthings.com/web-exclusives/2016/07/healing-through-repentance.

Gaillardetz, Richard R. *The Church in the Making: Lumen Gentium, Christus Dominus, Orientalium Ecclesiarum.* New York/Mahwah, NJ: Paulist Press, 2006.

Gaillardetz, Richard R. "Doctrinal Authority in the Francis Era." *Commonweal* (19 December 2016). www.commonwealmagazine.org/doctrinal-authority-francis-era.

Gaillardetz, Richard R. "In the Service of the People." *The Tablet* (16 April 2016): 6–8.

Gaillardetz, Richard R. "The Pastoral Orientation of Doctrine." In *Go Into the Streets! The Welcoming Church of Pope Francis*, edited by Richard R. Gaillardetz and Thomas Rausch, 125–140. New York: Paulist Press, 2016.

Gaillardetz, Richard R. *An Unfinished Council: Vatican II, Pope Francis, and the Renewal of Catholicism.* Collegeville, MN: Liturgical Press, 2015.

Gallagher, Raphael. "The Reception of *Amoris Laetitia*." *The Pastoral Review* 12/4 (July/August 2016): 4–9.

Goertz, Stephan and Caroline Witting, eds. *Amoris Laetitia: Wendepunkt in der Moraltheologie?* Freiburg: Herder, 2016.

Granados, José, Stephan Kampowski and Juan José Pérez-Soba. *Accompanying, Discerning, Integrating: A Handbook for the Pastoral Care of the Family According to* Amoris Laetitia. Translated by Michael J. Miller. Steubenville, OH: Emmaus Road Publishing, 2017.

Harmon, Catherine. "Make Sure You Read These Passages from Amoris Laetitia, Too." *The Catholic World Report* (8 April 2016). www.catholicworldreport.com/Blog/4701/make_sure_you_read_these_passages_from_iamoris_laetitiai_too.aspx.

Harrison, Brian W., O.S. "Authentic Confusion over Pope Francis' 'Authentic Magisterium'." *Life Site* (19 December 2017). www.lifesitenews.com/opinion/authentic-confusion-over-pope-francis-authentic-magisterium.

Healy, Nicholas J. "The Light of Faith and the Development of Doctrine." *Anthropotes* 22 (2017): 197–214.

Hickey, Margaret. "Amoris Laetitia: A Reflection." *The Furrow* 67/9 (September 2016): 482–485.

Hitchcock, James. *Catholicism and Modernity: Confrontation or Capitulation.* New York: Seabury Press, 1979.

Hitchens, Dan. "A Time of Crisis." *First Things* (30 October 2017). www.firstth ings.com/web-exclusives/2017/10/a-time-of-crisis.

Höllinger, Stephanie. "Do We Expect Too Much? A Reflection on Expectations and Marriage in *Amoris Laetitia.*" In *A Point of No Return? Amoris Laetitia on Marriage, Divorce and Remarriage,* 103–119.

Hughson, Thomas. "Interpreting Vatican II: 'A New Pentecost'." *Theological Studies* 69 (2008): 3–37.

Huizenga, Leroy. "The Joy of Love in the Hands of the Clergy." *The Catholic World Report* (8 April 2016). www.catholicworldreport.com/Item/4702/ithe_joy_of_ lovei_in_the_hands_of_the_clergy.aspx.

Imbelli, Robert P. "The Principled Ambivalence of Pope Francis." *First Things* (7November2017).www.firstthings.com/web-exclusives/2017/11/the-principled- ambivalence-of-pope-francis.

Ivereigh, Austen, ed. *Unfinished Journey: The Church 40 Years after Vatican II: Essays for John Wilkins.* New York/London: Continuum, 2003.

John Paul II, Pope. "Apostolic Exhortation on the Role of the Christian Family in the Modern World." In *Familiaris Consortio.* (22 November 1981). w2.vatican.va/ content/john-paul-ii/pl/apost_exhortations/documents/hf_jp-ii_exh_19811122_ familiaris-consortio.html.

John Paul II, Pope. "Encyclical Letter." In *Veritatis Splendor.* (6 August 1993). w2.vatican.va/content/john-paul-ii/en/encyclicals/documents/hf_jp-ii_enc_ 06081993_veritatis-splendor.html.

John XXIII, Pope. "Opening Speech to the Council, [Gaudet Mater Ecclesia]." In *The Documents of Vatican II,* edited by Walter M. Abbott, 710–719. New York: America Press, 1966.

Join-Lambert, Arnaud. "Accompanying, Discerning and Integrating the Fragility of Couples: Pastors and Theologians at a Crossroads." In *A Point of No Return? Amoris Laetitia on Marriage, Divorce and Remarriage,* 141–161.

Joy, John and Michael Sirilla. "On 'Authentic Magisterium' and the Acta Apostolicae Sedis." *OnePeterFive* (11 December 2017). https://onepeterfive.com/ep- 44-dr-john-joy-dr-michael-sirilla-authentic-magisterium-acta-apostolicae-sedis/.

Kampowski, Stephan. "In *Amoris Laetitia,* the Family Is an Opportunity, Not a Problem." *The Catholic World Report* (12 April 2016). www.catholicworldreport. com/Item/4717/In_iAmoris_Laetitiai_the_family_is_an_opportunity_not_a_ problem.aspx.

Kasper, Walter. "'Amoris Laetitia': Bruch Oder Aufbruch? Eine Nachlese." *Stimmen der Zeit* 234 (2016): 723–732.

Kasper, Walter. *The Gospel of the Family.* Translated by William Madges. Mahwah, NJ: Paulist Press, 2014.

Kasper, Walter. *Pope Francis' Revolution of Tenderness and Love: Theological and Pastoral Perspectives.* New York: Paulist Press, 2015.

Kasper, Walter. *Theology and Church.* New York: Crossroad, 1989.

Keenan, James F. "Receiving Amoris Laetitia." *Theological Studies* 78/1 (2017): 193–212.

Keller, Paul Jerome, O.P. "Is Spiritual Communion for Everyone?" *Nova et Vetera,* English Edition 12/3 (2014): 631–655.

Kelly, Conor M. "The Role of the Moral Theologian in the Church: A Proposal in the Light of *Amoris Laetitia.*" *Theological Studies* 77/4 (2016): 922–948.

Kilby, Karen. "Unfinished Business." *The Tablet* (16 April 2016): 8.

Knieps-Port le Roi, Thomas, ed. *A Point of No Return?* Amoris Laetitia *on Marriage, Divorce and Remarriage.* Berlin: Lit Verlag, 2017.

Knieps-Port le Roi, Thomas and Roger Burggraeve. "New Wine in New Wineskins: *Amoris Laetitia* and the Church's Teaching on Marriage and Family." *Louvain Studies* 39 (2015–2016): 284–302.

Komonchak, Joseph A. "Benedict XVI and the Interpretation of Vatican II." In *The Crisis of Authority in Catholic Modernity,* edited by Michael J. Lacy and Francis Oakley, 93–110. New York: Oxford Press, 2011.

Komonchak, Joseph A. "Interpreting the Council: Catholic Attitudes toward Vatican II." In *Being Right: Conservative Catholics in America,* edited by Mary Jo Weaver & R. Scott Appleby, 17–36. Bloomington: Indiana University Press, 1995.

Kuljovsky, Branislav. "The Law of Gradualness of the Gradualness of Law? A Critical Analysis of *Amoris Laetitia.*" In *A Point of No Return? Amoris Laetitia on Marriage, Divorce and Remarriage,* 45–64.

Lakeland, Paul. *A Council That Will Never End: Lumen Gentium and the Church Today.* Collegeville, MN: Liturgical Press, 2013.

Lamb, Christopher. "Compassion Is This Pastor's Watchword." *The Tablet* (16 April 2016): 4–5.

Lamb, Christopher. "Francis on the Front Foot." *The Tablet* (30 September 2017): 4–5.

Lamb, Matthew L. and Matthew Levering, eds. *Vatican II: Renewal within Tradition.* Oxford/New York: Oxford University Press, 2008.

Lane, Dermot A. "Vatican II: The Irish Experience." *The Furrow* 55/2 (February 2004): 67–81.

Les Evêques de Belgique. "*Amoris Laetitia*: Lettre pastorale." www.cathobel.be/wp-content/uploads/2017/05/2017-05-09-Amoris-laetitia-Lettre-pastorale.pdf.

Lindbeck, George. *The Future of Roman Catholic Theology: Vatican II-Catalyst for Change.* Philadelphia: Fortress, 1970.

Lindbeck, George. "A Protestant Point of View." In *Vatican II: An Interfaith Appraisal,* edited by John H. Miller, C.S.C., 219–230. Notre Dame, IN: University of Notre Dame Press, 1996.

Lintner, Martin M. "Divorce and Remarriage: A Reading of Amoris Laetitia from a Theological-Ethical Perspective." In *A Point of No Return? Amoris Laetitia on Marriage, Divorce and Remarriage,* 123–140.

Lopes, Steven J. *A Pledged Troth: A Pastoral Letter on* Amoris Laetitia. Heuston, TX: Personal Ordinariate of the Chair of Peter, 2016. https://ordinariate.net/letters-and-statements.

López, Rodrigo Guerra. "The Relevance of Some Reflections by Karol Wojtyła for Understanding *Amoris Laetitia*: Creative Fidelity." *L'Osservatore Romano* (22 July 2016). www.osservatoreromano.va/en/news/relevance-some-reflections-karol-wojtyla-understan.

Marchetto, Agostino. *The Second Vatican Ecumenical Council: A Counterpoint for the History of the Council.* Chicago, IL: University of Scranton Press, 2010.

Martin, James. "Dissent, Now & Then: Thomas Weinandy and the Meaning of Jesuit Discernment." *America* (3 November 2017). www.americamagazine.org/faith/2017/11/03/dissent-now-then-thomas-weinandy-and-meaning-jesuit-discernment.

Martin, James. "Understanding Discernment Is Key to Understanding 'Amoris Laetitia'." *America* (7 April 2016). www.americamagazine.org/issue/discernment-key-amoris-laetitia.

Marx, Reinhard. "Reflections on the Synod Process and *Amoris Laetitia*." In *A Point of No Return? Amoris Laetitia on Marriage, Divorce and Remarriage*, 11–19.

McCabe, Megan. "Pope Francis: We Must 'See in the Women's Movement the Working of the Spirit'." *America* (April 8, 2016). www.americamagazine.org/issue/article/francis-family-and-feminism.

McDermott, Gerald. "Is Pope Francis a Liberal Protestant?" *First Things* (15 November 2017). www.firstthings.com/web-exclusives/2017/11/is-pope-francis-a-liberal-protestant.

McElwee, Joshua J. "Prelates: Synod Document Is the Fruit of Vatican II Spirit." *National Catholic Reporter* (13 October 2014). www.ncronline.org/news/vatican/prelates-synod-document-fruit-vatican-ii-spirit.

Melina, Livio. "First Reflections on *Amoris Laetitia*." www.istitutogp2.it/public/Amoris%20Laetitia-Prime%20riflessioni%20%282016.04.12%29%20ING.pdf.

Mirus, Jeffrey. "The Acta Apostolicae Sedis Is Not an Exercise of the Magisterium of the Church." (19 December 2017). www.catholicculture.org/commentary/otc.cfm?id=1523.

Montagna, Diane. "Amoris Laetitia Uses Orthodoxy as 'Mask' to Conceal Moral Errors: Catholic Philosopher." *Life Site* (10 October 2017). www.lifesitenews.com/news/amoris-laetitia-uses-orthodoxy-as-mask-to-conceal-moral-errors-catholic-phi.

Montagna, Diane. "New Academy for Life Member Uses Amoris to Say Some Circumstances 'Require' Contraception." *Life Site* (8 January 2018). www.lifesitenews.com/news/new-academy-for-life-member-uses-amoris-to-say-some-circumstances-require-c.

Müller, Gerhard R. "Foreword to Rocco Buttiglione." *Riposte (amichevoli) ai critici di Amoris Laetitia.* (Milan: Ares, 2017). English translation provided by Vatican Insider. www.lastampa.it/2017/10/30/vaticaninsider/eng/the-vatican/communion-to-the-remarried-mller-there-can-be-mitigating-factors-in-guilt-OI0rK5MajqAn9gHGQE1YbO/pagina.html.

Müller, Gerhard R. "Testimony to the Power of Grace: On the Indissolubility of Marriage and the Debate Concerning the Civilly Remarried and the Sacraments." In *Remaining in the Truth of Christ: Marriage and Communion in the Catholic Church*, 148–165.

Müller, Gerhard R. "What Can We Expect from the Family?" Address at conciliar seminary of Oviedo. (4 May 2016). http://chiesa.espresso.repubblica.it/articolo/1351294bdc4.html?eng=y.

Nolan, Ann M.C. "Vatican II: Changing the Style of Being Church." *Australasian Catholic Record* 98/4 (October 2012): 397–407.

O'Collins, Gerald. "The Joy of Love (Amoris Laetitia): The Papal Exhortation in Its Context." *Theological Studies* 77 (2016): 905–921.

O'Connell, Gerard. "'Amoris Laetitia' Represents an Organic Development of Doctrine, 'Not a Rupture'." *America* (8 April 2016). www.americamagazine.org/faith/2016/04/08/amoris-laetitia-represents-organic-development-doctrine-not-rupture.

O'Hanlon, Gerry. "The Joy of Love-'*Amoris Laetitia*'." *The Furrow* 67/6 (June 2016): 328–336.

Olson, Carl E. "Francis' Sprawling Exhortation a Marriage of Profound and Muddles." *The Catholic World Report* (8 April 2016). www.catholicworldreport.com/Item/4698/francis_sprawling_exhortation_a_marriage_of_profound_and_muddled.aspx.

O'Malley, John. "Developments, Reforms and Two Great Reformations: Towards a Historical Assessment of Vatican II." *Theological Studies* 44 (1983): 373–406.

O'Malley, John. "Erasmus and Vatican II: Interpreting the Council." In *Cristianesimo nella storia: Saggi in onore di Giuseppe Alberigo*, edited by Alberto Melloni, Daniele Menozzi and Maria Paola Toschi, 195–211. Bologna: Il Mulino, 1996.

O'Malley, John. "'The Hermeneutic of Reform': A Historical Analysis." *Theological Studies* 73 (2012): 517–546.

O'Malley, John. "Misdirections: The Sure-Fire Ways to Mix Up the Teaching of Vatican II." *America* (4 February 2015): 25–27.

O'Malley, John. "Reform, Historical Consciousness, and Vatican II's Aggiornamento." *Theological Studies* 32 (1971): 573–601.

O'Malley, John. "The Style of Vatican II." *America* (24 February 2003): 12–15.

O'Malley, John. "Vatican II: Did Anything Happen?" *Theological Studies* 67 (2006): 3–33.

O'Malley, John. "Vatican II: Official Norms." *America* (31 March 2003): 11–14.

O'Malley, John. *What Happened at Vatican II*. Cambridge, MA/London: Harvard University Press, 2010.

Ormerod, Neil. "Vatican II: Continuity or Discontinuity? Toward an Ontology of Meaning," *Theological Studies* 71 (2010): 609–636.

Ouellet, Marc. "Accompanying, Discerning, Integrating Weakness." *L'Osservatore Romano* (21 November 2017). www.osservatoreromano.va/en/news/accompanying-discerning-integrating-weakness.

Ouellet, Marc. "A Missionary Gaze: Understanding 'Amoris Laetitia'." *L'Osservatore Romano* (8 November 2017). www.osservatoreromano.va/en/news/missionary-gaze.

Pentin, Edward N. "Full Text and Explanatory Notes of Cardinals' Questions on 'Amoris Laetitia'." *National Catholic Register* (14 November 2016). www.ncregister.com/blog/edward-pentin/full-text-and-explanatory-notes-of-cardinals-questions-on-amoris-laetitia.

Pentin, Edward N. *The Rigging of a Vatican Synod? An Investigation Into Alleged Manipulation at the Extraordinary Synod on the Family*. San Francisco: Ignatius Press, 2015.

Pérez-Soba Juan José and Stephan Kampowski. *The Gospel of the Family: Going Beyond Cardinal Kasper's Proposal in the Debate on Marriage, Civil Re-Marriage and Communion in the Church*. Translated by Michael J. Miller. San Francisco: Ignatius Press, 2014.

Pesch, Otto Herman. *The Second Vatican Council: Prehistory-Event-Results-Posthistory.* Translated by Deirdre Dempsey. Milwaukee, WI: Marquette University Press 2014.

Peters, Edward N. "First thoughts on the English Version of Pope Francis' *Amoris Laetitia.*" *The Catholic World Report* (8 April 2016). www.catholicworldreport. com/Blog/4699/dr_edward_peters_first_thoughts_on_the_english_version_of_ pope_francis_amoris_laetitia.aspx.

Peters, Edward N. "The Law Before 'Amoris' Is the Law After." *The Catholic World Report* (10 April 2016). www.catholicworldreport.com/Blog/4708/the_law_before_ amoris_is_the_law_after.aspx.

Peters, Edward N. "Pope Francis' Letter to the Argentine Bishops is in the Acta Apostolicae Sedis: Now What?" *The Catholic World Report* (4 December 2017). www.catholicworldreport.com/2017/12/04/pope-francis-letter-to-the-argentine-bishops-is-in-the-acta-apostolicae-sedis-now-what/.

Petrà, Basilio. "From *Familiaris Consortio* to *Amoris Laetitia*: Continuity of the Pastoral Attitude and a Step Forward." *INTAMS Review* 22: 202–216. Doi: 10.2143/ INT.22.2.3194501.

Pierantoni, Claudio. "Josef Seifert, Pure Logic, and the Beginning of the Official Persecution of Orthodoxy within the Church." *Aemaet* 6/2 (2017): 22–33. http:// aemaet.de urn:nbn:de:0288–20130928711.

Pollitt, Russell. "Bishops of South Africa Welcome Pope Francis' Exhortation." *America* (8 April 2016). www.americamagazine.org/content/dispatches/popes-exhortation-welcomed-south-africa.

Pongratz-Lippitt, Christa. "German Group at Family Synod Finds Their Suggestions in Pope's Exhortation." *National Catholic Reporter* (15 April 2016). www. ncronline.org/news/vatican/german-group-family-synod-finds-their-suggestions-popes-exhortation.

Pongratz-Lippitt, Christa. "'Synodality Must Once Again Become a Structural Practice in the Church', German Cardinals and Theologians Insist." *National Catholic Reporter* (15 December 2015). www.ncronline.org/blogs/ncr-today/ synodality-must-once-again-become-structural-practice-church-german-cardinals-and.

Pontifical Council for Legislative Texts. "II. Concerning the Admission to Holy Communion of Faithfull Who Are Divorced and Remarried." (24 June 2000).www. vatican.va/roman_curia/pontifical_councils/intrptxt/documents/rc_pc_intrptxt_ doc_20000706_declaration_en.html.

Pottmeyer, Herman J. "A New Phase in the Reception of Vatican II: Twenty Years of Interpretation of the Council." In *The Reception of Vatican II*, edited by Giuseppe Alberigo, Jean-Pierre Jossua and Joseph A. Komonchak, 27–43. Washington, DC: Catholic University of America Press, 1987.

Poulat, Emile. *Une Eglise ébranlée: Chamgement, conflit et continuité de Pie XII à Jean Paul II.* Paris: Casterman, 1980.

Radcliffe, Timothy, O.P. "How Can We 'Make Room for the Consciences of the Faithful'?" In *A Point of No Return? Amoris Laetitia on Marriage, Divorce and Remarriage*, 65–73.

74   *Bibliography*

Ratzinger, Joseph. *Principles of Catholic Theology: Building Stones for a Fundamental Theology*. Translated by Sister Mary Frances McCarthy, S.N.D. San Francisco: Ignatius Press, 1987.

Ratzinger, Joseph. *Theological Highlights of Vatican II*. New York/Mahwah, NJ: Paulist Press, 2009 (Reprinted from 1966).

Ratzinger, Joseph. "VII. Fortieth Anniversary of the Constitution on the Sacred Liturgy: A Look Back and a Look Forward." In *Joseph Ratzinger, Theology of the Liturgy: The Sacramental Foundation of Christian Existence*, edited by Michael J. Miller. Translated by Kenneth Baker, S.J., Henry Taylor, et al., 574–588. San Francisco: Ignatius Press, 2014.

Ratzinger, Joseph and Vittorio Messori. *The Ratzinger Report: An Exclusive Interview on the State of the Church*. Translated by Salvator Attanasio and Graham Harrison. SanFrancisco: Ignatius Press, 1985.

Reese, Thomas J. "How Can the Church and Laity Work together to Promote 'Amoris Laetitia'?" *America* 217/11 (13 November 2017): 1–3.

Reese, Thomas J. "Synod on Remarried Catholics, Consensus in Ambiguity." *National Catholic Reporter* (14 October 2015). www.ncronline.org/blogs/faith-and-justice/synod-remarried-catholics-consensus-ambiguity.

Richard, Lucien, Daniel T. Harrington and John W. O'Malley, eds. *Vatican II, The Unfinished Agenda: A Look to the Future*. New York: Paulist Press, 1987.

Rowland, Tracey. *Catholic Theology*. London/New York: Bloomsbury/T & T Clark, 2017.

Rowland, Tracey. *Ratzinger's Faith: The Theology of Pope Benedict XVI*. Oxford: University Press, 2008.

Routhier, Gilles. "Vatican II: Relevance and Future." *Theological Studies* 74 (2013): 537–554.

Rovati, Alessandro. "Mercy Is a Person: Pope Francis and the Christological Turn in Moral Theology." *Journal of Moral Theology* 6/2 (2017): 48–69.

Rush, Ormond. *Still Interpreting Vatican II: Some Hermeneutical Principles*. New York: Paulist Press, 2004.

Sagandoy, Vincent Mynem C. "Canonical Imperatives of Pastoral Care in Amoris Laetitia Concerning Catholics with Irregular Marital Status." In *A Point of No Return? Amoris Laetitia on Marriage, Divorce and Remarriage*, 181–194.

Salzman, Todd A. and Michael G. Lawler. "Amoris Laetitia and Catholic Morals." *The Furrow* 67/12 (December 2016): 666–675.

Salzman, Todd A. and Michael G. Lawler. "*Amoris Laetitia* and the Development of Catholic Theological Ethics: A Reflection." In *A Point of No Return? Amoris Laetitia on Marriage, Divorce and Remarriage*, 30–44.

Salzman, Todd A. and Michael G. Lawler. "In Amoris Laetitia, Francis' Model of Conscience Empowers Catholics." *National Catholic Reporter* (7 September 2016). www.ncronline.org/news/theology/amoris-laetitia-francis-model-conscience-empowers-catholics.

Sample, Alexander K. *Pastoral Letter on the Reading of* Amoris Laetitia *in Light of Church Teaching: 'A True and Living Icon'*. Portland, OR: Archdiocese of Portland, 2016. http://archdpdx.org/documents/2016/10/PASTORAL%20LETTER%20A%20True%20and%20Living%20Icon%20FINAL-1.pdf.

Scicluna, Charles J. and Mario Grech (Bishops of Malta). *Criteria for the Application of Chapter VIII of Amoris Laetitia*. Malta/Gozo: Archdiocese of Malta/ Diocese of Gozo, 2017. http://ms.maltadiocese.org/WEBSITE/2017/PRESS%20 RELEASES/Norms%20for%20the%20Application%20of%20Chapter%20 VIII%20of%20AL.pdf.

Schloesser, Stephen. "Against Forgetting: Memory, History, Vatican II." *Theological Studies* 67 (2006): 275–319.

Schökel Alonso and María Bravo. *A Manual of Hermeneutics*. Translated by Brook W.R. Pearson. New York/Sheffield, UK: Sheffield Academic Press, 1998.

Schönborn, Christian. "Intervention at Presentation of Amoris Laetitia." (19 March 2016). http://press.vatican.va/content/salastampa/it/bollettino/pubblico/2016/04/ 08/0241/00531.html#ens.

Schönborn, Christian and Antonio Spadaro. "The Demands of Love." *America* (15–22 August 2016). www.americamagazine.org/issue/demands-love.

"Second Vatican Council, Constitution on the Sacred Liturgy *Sacrosanctum Concilium*." (4 December 1963). www.vatican.va/archive/hist_councils/ii_vatican_council/ documents/vat-ii_const_19631204_sacrosanctum-concilium_en.html.

"Second Vatican Council, Pastoral Constitution on the Church in the Modern World *Gaudium et spes*." (7 December 1965). www.vatican.va/archive/hist_councils/ ii_vatican_council/documents/vat-ii_const_19651207_gaudium-et-spes_en. html.

Seifert, Josef. "Amoris Laetitia: Joy, Sadness and Hopes." *Aemaet* 5/2 (2016): 160– 249. http://aemaet.de urn:nbn:de:0288-2015080654.

Seifert, Josef. "Does Pure Logic Threaten to Destroy the Entire Moral Doctrine of the Catholic Church?" *Aemaet* 6/2 (2017): 2–9. http://aemaet.deurn:nbn:de: 0288-20130928692.

Seifert, Josef. "The Persecution of Orthodoxy." *First Things* (5 October 2017). www. firstthings.com/web-exclusives/2017/10/the-persecution-of-orthodoxy.

Simmonds, Gemma. "Amoris Laetitia: A View from the Female Bridge." *Thinking Faith* (13 May 2016). www.thinkingfaith.org/articles/amoris-laetitia-%E2%80% 93-view-female-bridge.

Spadaro, Antonio and Louis J. Cameli. "Watching for God." *America* (1–8 August 2016): 24–27.

Spinello, Richard A. "On Rocco Buttiglione's Defense of Amoris Laetitia." *Crisis Magazine* (9 August 2016). www.crisismagazine.com/2016/rocco-buttiglliones-defense-amoris-laetitia.

Steinfels, Peter. *A People Adrift: The Crisis of the Roman Catholic Church in America*. New York: Simon & Schuster, 2003.

Stenfels, Peter, Paige E. Hochschild, William L. Portier, Sandra Yocum and George Dennis O'Brien. "A Balancing Act: Reading 'Amoris Laetitia'." *Commonweal* (20 May 2016): 13–21.

Strynkowski, John J. "An Open Letter to Father Weinandy, from His Predecessor, on 'Amoris Laetitia' and Pope Francis." *America* (2 November 2017). www.ameri camagazine.org/faith/2017/11/02/open-letter-father-weinandy-his-predecessor-amoris-laetitia-and-pope-francis.

Synod of Bishops. "Final Report." *Origins* 15 (1985): 445–446.

Tagle, Louis. "The Spirit of the Synod Is a Spirit of Listening." *Salt and Light Media* (15 October 2014). http://saltandlighttv.org/blogfeed/getpost.php?id=59095& language.

Taylor, Aaron. "Revelation on Tap: Vatican I and the 'Amoris Laetitia' Controversy." *First Things* (25 August 2017). www.firstthings.com/web-exclusives/2017/08/revelation-on-tap-vatican-i-and-the-amoris-laetitia-controversy.

Tetlow, Joseph A. *Ignatius Loyola: Spiritual Exercises*. New York: Crossroad, 1992.

Tornielli, Andrea. "Pope Francis: The New John XXIII?" *La Stampa* (3 June 2013). www.lastampa.it/2013/06/03/esteri/vatican-insider/en/pope-francis-the-new-john-xxiii-O5YQamutYpzvELP3YcEBAJ/pagina.html.

Vallini, Agostino. *"La letizia dell'amore": il cammino delle famiglie a Roma Relazione del Cardinale Vicario*. Diocesi di Roma: Convegno Pastorale, 2016.

Walford, Stephen. "Amoris Laetitia: The Questions That Really Need Answers." *La Stampa* (27 March 2017). www.lastampa.it/2017/03/27/vaticaninsider/eng/documents/amoris-laetitia-the-questions-that-really-need-answers-ppy8l1yk7em PPR7TUYrjQN/pagina.html.

Walford, Stephen. "Amoris Laetitia: Where Truth and Mercy Embrace: An Editorial on Apostolic Exhortation." *La Stampa* (22 January 2017). www.lastampa.it/2017/01/22/vaticaninsider/eng/documents/amoris-laetitia-where-truth-and-mercy-embrace-j7Wra0gHXbMppRm8A7CsRL/pagina.html.

Walford, Stephen. "The Magisterium of Pope Francis: His Predecessors Come to His Defence." *La Stampa* (7 February 2017). www.lastampa.it/2017/02/07/vaticaninsider/eng/the-vatican/the-magisterium-of-pope-francis-his-predecessors-come-to-his-defence-x5jzE4YtghvlnRvSvcolGM/pagina.html.

Walford, Stephen. "Open Letter to the Four Dubia Cardinals." *La Stampa* (27 June 2017). www.lastampa.it/2017/06/27/vaticaninsider/eng/documents/open-letter-to-the-four-dubia-cardinals-nIsyPMFIjp2M5wjLZ1CHJO/pagina.html.

Weinandy, Thomas G. "Letter to Pope Francis." (31 July 2017). https://cruxnow.com/wp-content/uploads/2017/10/Francis-Letter-Final.pdf.

Whitehead, Kenneth. "Vatican II Then and Now: A Review Essay on John O'Malley, S.J.'s *What Happened at Vatican II*." *Nova et Vetera, English Edition* 8/2 (2010): 467–483.

Worgul, George S. "*Amoris Laetitia*: On the Need for a Contextual Theology and Inculturation in Practice." In *A Point of No Return? Amoris Laetitia on Marriage, Divorce and Remarriage*, 20–29.

Index